And People?

Or

**Why Are Managers' Cars the
Most Important Asset in Every Organization?**

Ivica Vrančić

Technics Publications

Published by:

2 Lindsley Road
Basking Ridge, NJ 07920 USA

https://www.TechnicsPub.com

First Printing 2015

Copyright © 2015 by Ivica Vrančić

ISBN: 9781634620772

Library of Congress Control Number: 2015936518

The blame for this book lies with T.I.N.A.:

I. is to be blamed because he took away a lot of free time to write and create the book

T., N. and A. are to be blamed because they gave I. the time needed to create the book

But they were also the greatest possible support

T., N. and A., I love you more than anything in this world

Table of Contents

FOREWORD BY DAVE ULRICH   **3**

INTRODUCTION   **7**

ONE: TO LEAD PEOPLE OR TO MANAGE PEOPLE, OR TO LEAD
AND TO MANAGE PEOPLE   **11**

LEADERSHIP   **12**

WHAT IS LEADERSHIP?   **15**

LEADERSHIP AND MANAGEMENT   **18**

EXAMPLES, TOOLS, AND RESEARCH   **24**

    LEADERSHIP AND TRUST   24

LEADERSHIP ISSUE OF TODAY   **25**

TWO: MOTIVATING PEOPLE   **27**

BASIC THEORETICAL CONCEPTS   **29**

    HERTZBERG   30

    MASLOW   30

    RECOGNIZING A JOB WELL DONE   35

    COMMUNICATION   36

    ACKNOWLEDGING INVESTED EFFORT WITHOUT REGARD TO RESULTS   37

    SETTING GOALS   37

    A FEELING OF INCLUSION   38

    PURPOSE AND CONTEXT   38

THE SIGNIFICANCE OF MONEY FOR MOTIVATION   **39**

CEO AND "TYPICAL" WORKER COMPENSATION IN THE ORGANIZATION   **42**

THE ROLE OF PUNISHMENT   **43**

LIFE-WORK BALANCE, NOT *WORK-LIFE* BALANCE   **45**

EXAMPLES, TOOLS, AND RESEARCH   **51**

    MCKINSEY'S RESEARCH   51

THREE: OUR BEHAVIORS, OUR (ORGANIZATIONAL) CULTURE 55

THE EMERGENCE AND STRUCTURE OF ORGANIZATIONAL CULTURE 58

THE POWER OF ORGANIZATIONAL CULTURE 64

ORGANIZATIONAL CULTURE AND BUSINESS RESULTS 66

ORGANIZATIONAL CULTURE MANAGEMENT, ALTERATION AND

MAINTENANCE 67

REPLACEMENT OF THE MAIN PERSON IN CHARGE 68

"PULLING IN" AND INCLUDING OTHER QUIET PEOPLE FROM THE

COMPANY 69

THE SELECTION OF NEW AND DIFFERENT PEOPLE 70

A CHANGE IN THE REWARD SYSTEM AND/OR PROCEDURES AND

PROCESSES 71

CULTURE SHOCK 72

SYSTEMATICALLY WORKING ON VALUES 73

RECOGNITION AND EVALUATION OF DESIRED BEHAVIORS 75

ORGANIZATIONAL CULTURE MEASUREMENT 77

EXAMPLES, TOOLS, AND RESEARCH 82

KOTTER ABOUT ORGANIZATIONAL CULTURE 82

THE INFLUENCE OF THE LEADER'S PERSONAL VALUES ON

ORGANIZATIONAL CULTURE AND THE ORGANIZATION'S RESULTS 83

CREATION OF A TAILOR-MADE OR ORGANIZATION-SPECIFIC SET OF

INSTRUMENTS AND TOOLS FOR ORGANIZATIONAL CULTURE

MEASUREMENT AND MANAGEMENT 87

FOUR: ATTRACTING, RECRUITING AND SELECTING THE PEOPLE FOR US 93

ATTRACTING THE CANDIDATES—*TO ATTRACT* 94

WHERE ARE THE PEOPLE? LACK OF PEOPLE 94

EMPLOYEE VALUE PROPOSITION (EVP) 97

EMPLOYER BRANDING 104

GATHERING INFORMATION ABOUT JOB CANDIDATES—*TO RECRUIT* 107

SOURCES OF INFORMATION ABOUT THE CANDIDATES 110

RESUME (CV) 110

EMPLOYMENT AGENCIES 110

RECOMMENDATIONS 112

FACEBOOK, TWITTER, OR LINKEDIN 112

SELECTION OF CANDIDATES AND FUTURE EMPLOYEES IN THE

ORGANIZATION—TO SELECT 115

SELECTION TECHNIQUES AND METHODS 121

RESUMES (CVS) 121

APPLICATION FORMS 123

PSYCHOMETRIC MEASURING (TESTS AND QUESTIONNAIRES) 123

INTERVIEWS 125

ASSESSMENT CENTERS 129

EXAMPLES, TOOLS, AND RESEARCH 132

THE TOWERS WATSON STUDY 132

KEY FINDINGS 132

THE UNIVERSUM STUDY 134

METHODS OF SELECTION—PREDICTION VALIDITY 135

INVOLVEMENT OF THE ORGANIZATION'S EMPLOYEES IN THE SELECTION

PROCESS 136

THE STAR TECHNIQUE IN CONDUCTING A SELECTION INTERVIEW 136

FIVE: DEVELOPING OUR PEOPLE 141

ENVIRONMENT AND DEVELOPMENT 147

COMPETENCE AS A BASIS FOR DEVELOPMENT 152

DETERMINING DEVELOPMENTAL NEEDS 156

DEVELOPMENTAL TECHNIQUES AND TOOLS 165

DEVELOPMENT ≠ TRAINING 166

SPECIAL FORMS OF DEVELOPMENT—MENTORING AND COACHING 179

MENTORING 179

COACHING 180

WHEN TO USE COACHING 183

HOW TO CONDUCT COACHING 185

COACHING AS A CYCLE/PROCESS/METHOD 186

FEEDBACK 188

Talents: Recognition and Development   191

Techniques of Assessing the Success of Development—Measures

of Success   194

    Baseline Measurement—The Starting Point   195

    Levels of Measuring Development   195

    Measuring Satisfaction with Developmental Activities   196

    Measuring the Adopted or New Knowledge   196

    Measuring Changes in Behavior—Actual Development   197

    Measuring Business Results as a Measure of Development   198

Examples, Tools, and Research   202

    CIPD research   202

    Making coaching work   202

    Coaching as a System within an Organization   203

    Building a "pathway" to leadership   206

SIX: TO MANAGE PEOPLE BY MIND AND TO LEAD THEM BY

EMOTION   209

REFERENCES   215

INDEX   219

Acknowledgements

Some believe it is only great power that can hold evil in check. But that is not what I have found. I have found that it is small everyday deeds of ordinary folk that keep the darkness at bay. Small acts of kindness and love.

Gandalf, *The Lord of the Rings*

This book was created not with the help of *great power*, but over the course of several years through daily *deeds*, and based on twenty years of experience. Even though it's possible that many of you will regard it as an expert book, it is primarily an experience book.

It was created long before the writing began; it was created on the first day of my experience in working with people. It is based on all my attempts and mistakes and learning, which sooner or later come back to the fact that you cannot use any great power with people, or even yourself, but that you can succeed with small human expressions of *kindness and love*. Its basic source is experience, particularly my exchange of experience with numerous people. It would certainly look different had, along the way of its creation, kindness and love not been unselfishly shared by Tom Bunjevac (who taught me that life is much wider and deeper than any profession, even psychology), Vera Franc (who taught me the first steps of what is today called Human Resources Management), Borna Zane and Vinko Dumičić (who each in their own way taught me a human approach in the merciless business environment), and Bruno Filipi (who helped me understand why the business environment needs people). THANK YOU.

Foreword by Dave Ulrich

Leading and Managing ... People and Organization ... Through Human Resources

Sometimes being successful in business feels complex. Leaders get inundated with innumerable tools for success including visions, goals, strategies, values, capabilities, competencies, initiatives, programs, processes, and priorities. When overwhelmed, leaders sometimes tune out ideas that would have impact because they can not simplify and synthesize those ideas.

Ivica does a masterful job in this well written book of simplifying the complex requirements for business success. The following figure shows my summary of his excellent work:

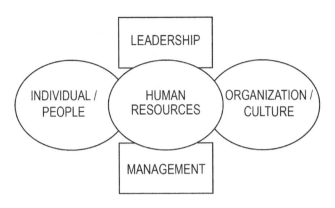

First, business success comes from having both leaders and managers. Thoughtful colleagues have made the distinction between leaders and managers. Managers do things right; leaders do the right things. Managers deliver in the present; leaders create the future. Managers command and control; leaders coach and communicate. Managers solve problems; leaders identify problems. Managers react; leaders anticipate. And so forth.

Ivica captures these differences in very pragmatic and useful ways. He offers metaphors and examples of how leadership and management skills both need to exist in a successful business. His insights are particularly helpful in that he adapts them to his experiences in Eastern Europe, yet shows how they would apply to businesses throughout the world.

Second, he discusses two primary outcomes where leaders and managers must focus: individual and organization. He does a very thoughtful job talking about how people make up an organization, but an organization is more than the individual people. On the people side, he synthesizes work by people management thought leaders on issues of motivation, personal growth, and work/life (or life/work balance). On the organization or culture side, he does a wonderful job laying out what is meant by culture, how to build a culture, and how to ensure the continuity of the right culture.

Third, he proposes a set of human resource tools around sourcing and developing people. These tools enable managers and leaders to ensure a stable flow of people and the creation of the right culture.

This three-step logic and elegantly simple flow offer readers a number of useful insights into how to ensure business success.

The book does a wonderful job with simplicity and clarity. Ivica distils volumes of management ideas into digestible nuggets that can be used. He then brings in research from thought leaders with specific findings and approaches that inform choices. He offers examples that bring the ideas to life.

He also makes sure that the reader is responsible to manage the tensions or tradeoffs between leadership and management, between individuals and organizations. Creating and sustaining a successful business is not a linear progression following a how-to guide. Success comes from navigating a more complex set of choices. Ivica offers a thoughtful roadmap that can be used to help executives at any level of a company make informed choices about building a successful organization.

Introduction

"People are our greatest asset; they are our most important resource and greatest value"

Y ou have probably heard this lie many times in your life, while your back may bear the experience of its real meaning.

At the same time, when you ask the leading people in any organization about the greatest asset they have, without pausing (and maybe without thinking, either?) they will answer with that sentence.

Those same leading people will, in periods of less success, unrealized results or what is recognized as a crisis by the business world, give up that greatest value first. They will do it in various ways: by reducing the total numbers of that greatest value (or, as some comfortingly call it, "optimization," or more directly "downsizing"), by additional pressure on and exhaustion of that greatest value, etc., instead of by investing in its development.

On the other hand, those same leading people will actually still be focused on the real greatest value—managers' cars.

Under no circumstances will they stop investing in the development of their cars (a new GPS is certainly welcome, while the maintenance frequency will certainly not be reduced); naturally, they will in no way make the downsizing happen in their car park (for example, from a 7 Series to a 5 Series, from an S-Class to an E-Class, or from an A8 to an A6), and certainly will not exhaust them fully—because, for goodness sake, policies and procedures clearly state that after 120,000 miles or three years they will get a new, more advanced and better car.

They will query and complain about why a certain service related to people is expensive (development, protective gear, health checks), but they will accept without reservation the prices offered for even the most expensive cars, just to drive them.

The greatest value of an organization—i.e. people—is usually posted in financial reports under expenses (we have no intention here to discuss bookkeeping/accounting principles, but to emphasize the reality and illogicality of observing people as the most valuable resource), and that includes not only their salaries and tangibles, but also the element related to talent development.

The "real" greatest values, managers' cars, are usually purchased by opening a kind of OPEX or CAPEX, i.e. a kind of investment, an increase of value in those same books.

Expenses are, at least nowadays, simply cut off and reduced, and companies can most simply get rid of the "greatest expense" in their profit and loss accounts by laying people off: but what, then, about the company's greatest value?

In the processes of guiding and managing people, what is very often applied is a mechanical approach and a "copy-and-paste" concept of managing other types of processes and resources within an organization (e.g. quality processes, manufacture, warehousing, expenses and finances, sales, marketing...). But such a mechanical approach to management is not possible, or at least not sufficient or appropriate when it comes to people, as the real and greatest value of a company.

There are at least two reasons why it is not possible. These reasons will not be directly and explicitly mentioned throughout this book, but we believe that what you will read between the covers of this book will provide at least some additional explanation of why to act differently with people.

This book does not intend to provide the answer on the following pages, certainly not a definitive one, because it is more focused on thinking about people, people management and people guidance (in the most positive meaning of that word), created as a result of extensive practice and the opportunity to see hundreds of managers in their managerial and leadership roles and numerous discussions with them, and dozens of various organizations, the people in them and their behaviors.

This book intends to be cynical when it comes to management's attitude towards their business cars, but it is more ambitious about being serious when talking about people and human value, which should truly be the greatest and most important value of each organization.

It is intended for all those driving managerial cars, and particularly and primarily for those who lead people and manage people within a business environment.

One

To Lead People or to Manage People, or to Lead and to Manage People

either they notice nothing...
or only count mistakes...
honestly I don't know...what is worse...
Ambitious...but not alert...
Loud...but not clear...
Aggressive...but not courageous...
You are awakening in vain..!!!

Goribor, a Serbian indie and alternative rock band

Instead of being courageous, clear and alert, they are aggressive, loud and ambitious, and rarely or never notice the good, but immediately notice the wrong.

Naturally, that does not happen to you, reading these lines, and does not describe you, but someone else, and it certainly describes your boss.

Leadership

The lyrics of Goribor describe, in the best possible way, an everyday and rather usual style of managing and leading people. They describe what every person can experience first-hand daily, and which can actually be described as anti-leadership or anti-management. So what is leadership, and what is management?

The story of leadership must be as old as humanity itself, and it has been especially and intensively discussed and studied in the last hundred years. It has become a part of the colloquial, the everyday and the prosaic, about which everyone has something to say. Everyone understands it, and everyone thinks they have the best solution.

On the other hand, it is one of the most studied and analyzed fields within organizational behavior, sociology, and psychology. Even if not the most significant, it is surely one of the most attractive areas for organizational theoreticians. Although so attractive and discussed and studied so much, leadership has remained a field without a definitive answer as to what it is, where its secret lies or how to advance it. Studies thus far have resulted in numerous models, theories, and concepts (some of which expired even before the ink dried), while others still hold true at least partially despite their date of creation and successfully describe elements of leadership.

Moses, Jesus Christ, Julius Caesar, Cleopatra, Genghis Khan, Muhammad, Christopher Columbus, Napoleon, Abraham Lincoln, Golda Meir, Mahatma Gandhi, Martin Luther King, Margaret Thatcher, John Paul II, Lee Iacocca, Anita Roddick, Steve Jobs, Dražen Petrović; but also Adolf Hitler, Benito Mussolini, and Joseph Stalin. These are all people who have managed to draw a large following, and very successfully at that, and to realize their set goals, be it groups they headed, organizations, racial groups, or entire peoples.

What would be the psychological profile of Jesus Christ if we were able to determine it with psychometric methods? Would Christopher Columbus have made it to America if he had used a different approach or if he had been a different individual? What was it about fragile and seemingly unsightly Gandhi that enabled him to succeed in leading the entire Indian people in the successful pursuit of freedom? What did Martin Luther King dream that made so many black Americans, and not only them, follow him? Does the secret of Lee Iacocca's success lie in his famous claim: "You can take all my factories and plants, all my technology, but leave me my people, they are my wealth"? Would the Croatian national basketball team be more successful had Dražen Petrović lived longer, and not only because of his undeniable skills as a player, but because he was a real and undisputed leader who, many agree, left the team short-handed? And what was it about Hitler, Mussolini, and Stalin that meant they succeeded in drawing millions of followers despite their immoral, unethical, and overall negative methods and goals?

How is it that we all know who Lincoln, Roosevelt, and Kennedy were, while few of us recall Buchanan, Harding, and Coolidge? All were American presidents. Why is it we remember some, and not the others? Were the first more successful leaders?

The successes of the notorious Nazi general Erwin Rommel, the Desert Fox of North African battlefields, are attributed to his constant presence on the front line. Unlike federal generals, he was always on the front line, amongst his soldiers where he was at the source of information, thus making decisions based on direct knowledge. On the other hand, unlike his "colleagues," he consciously put himself at risk. Napoleon once proclaimed that an army of rabbits led by a lion would be more successful than an army of lions led by a rabbit. Does this idea of courage and readiness to expose oneself to risk apply to social, political, and economic environments? Researchers in the field think so. Many authors say that individuals who want to successfully lead others and accomplish their set goals must know how to recognize the situation and the people they want to lead towards that goal and adopt an appropriate attitude towards them.

The word "leadership" evokes very high associations and is tied to the aforementioned individuals, who are considered quality leaders for a reason.

But what does such an association signify to a team leader, a shift manager, a store manager, a head of any organizational unit, or the head of any company when they are required to be better leaders? Naturally, they can and must be leaders at each level, and many want to be, but what should they do, how should they act, and how can they develop their potential so as to succeed? In order for any manager of any organizational unit and at any company to develop in that direction, he or she must ask a simple question: *Why would someone follow me?*

Asking this question is a crucial, Copernican shift when it comes to leadership. It is not a sport in which one wins if one primarily disregards thinking about those who should follow. Leadership is a very tough and active contact sport where—of course—you win if you train and develop yourself. But in no way can you win if you do not think about the other side, perhaps more so than in any other contact sport. However, the other side is not and cannot be your enemy, but may become the greatest enemy if they do not want to follow you.

And, perhaps most importantly, leadership is not given but acquired, and in order to acquire it you must once again think about the other side.

Leadership is primarily a skill of influence, by which you get the other side to do what you want and what you think is the best and most correct choice. For the purpose of influence, some will use power, others knowledge, still others skill, experience, charisma, seniority, fear, reward, creation, authority, etc., but only if they understand or at least sense the way in which they must influence so as to succeed.

What is leadership?

The previous discussion in a way also represents the definition of leadership which could, in a very general sense, read: Leadership is every attempt to exert influence over another person to do what the leader considers necessary. Leadership is, therefore, a skill of influence, an interpersonal skill of exerting influence over another person. Therefore, in order to understand leadership, it is essential to stop and think of the other side— the follower, the person intended to be led. For each leader, this should be the center of development and the main focus of direction.

What has proven itself necessary and useful in leadership is understanding the other side, not just in a simple emotional and psychological sense, but understanding the other side for the sake of quality influence over them, and understanding what will bring the other side into a position to do in the best and most efficient way what the leader considers it most necessary to do.

Since leadership is primarily the skill of influencing the other side, the key question is about which process of influence leads or can lead people; it is precisely this question that discussions on leadership fail to ultimately answer. Previous discussions, theories, or models have, in various ways and through various strategies of influence, tried to or are trying to explain the basis of leadership. The majority of them—including both the oldest and most contemporary approaches—try to find the key to successful leadership in specific and certain personality traits (the traits of an individual), and it was long considered that successful people were of higher intelligence, emotionally more stable, socially more sensitive, etc.

A significant number of approaches tried to describe successful leadership through specific types of behavior (most often framed in forms of two-way and one-way communication); some approaches tried to define leadership by the powers possessed by individuals and how they used those powers. This approach ties into similar approaches that appraise or perceive successful leadership through various forms of authority (the authority of knowledge, the authority of the individual, the authority of experience, the authority of behavior, the authority of position). The natural continuation of these approaches is the models and theories that have tried to describe leadership through charisma, although they too have failed to provide an answer as it very soon became clear that charisma in itself is a problematic notion difficult to define.

A large proportion of leadership approaches and models, especially those aimed at a business environment, have tried to describe leadership as a specific behavior defined by two variables: behavior aimed at the task and behavior aimed at people. Newer theories return yet again to descriptions of specific characteristics of leaders—noting, for example, empathy as a key characteristic of leadership, or other forms of emotional and social sensitivity—while others discuss a leadership that is the quality result of caring for private and personal burdens (a balance between the private and professional).

Each of these approaches has contributed to an explanation of leadership, but none has managed to completely and fully explain the complexity of the term. Although not the most attractive, the most practical and most often used approaches to leadership in managerial development and education would be those describing leadership as a specific behavior determined by the variables of one's orientation to the task and the variable of one's orientation to a person (follower) who has to accomplish the task. Although criticized for being too simple and banal, these models and approaches have proven most useful when it comes to managerial education in the field of leadership.

At this point, it is worth mentioning morality and ethics as elements of leadership because history (as well as the present) clearly indicates that one can successfully influence people— lead them—while at the same time not being a moral person and not doing it in an ethical way. Leadership is not, it would seem, as romantic a position as it is often considered and discussed because clearly immoral and unethical people are or were supreme leaders (the leaders of mafia, terrorist or political groups or movements, as well as certain business leaders) and managed to or are still managing to influence others more than successfully.

Along with all that has been mentioned and studied so far, it would appear that the concept of leadership has changed or even become more complex in previous years. Events in North Africa, various social or socio-economic rebellions, movements such as Anonymous, and environmental actions are redefining the concept of leadership so that it is ceasing to be a psycho-social category that can be defined, as almost all approaches until now have been, through the personification of one person (his or her behavior, personality traits, values, charisma, and power). It is rather becoming a socio-social category in which no one person, leader, or head exists.

The role until now personified through the individual is now assumed by the group (not even a clearly defined team), which in its structure, way of action, and composition is unstable and inconsistent, even elusive. Even when a person who wants to assume the role of leader appears, they are removed and dethroned by the group; the person's influence is minimized, the group being the one that continues leading. Is this the process of creating something theoretically known as a self-leading group, a self-leading organization or even a self-leading society, or is the perception of leadership and current events surrounding it too idealistic, even utopian?

Leadership and Management

"Management" or "manager" is a formal position, defined by organizational structure and described as part of the process and/or responsibility tied to completing business processes. It is therefore simplest to define a manager as any person who manages at least one business process and/or one person. Such a definition covers a much wider population within the organization than one may consider in discussing management and when the very top or upper echelons of the hierarchal pyramid within organizations is considered.

Management is, simply put, a craft, one that has these basic activities and/or responsibilities:

- **Managing processes.** Responsibility for good, efficient and purposeful processes, their inputs and outputs, tools used, dynamics, and fluidity.
- **Managing products/services.** Responsibility for products or services produced as a result of the work of organizational units or processes. Therefore, this includes not only final products and services used by external clients, but also those used by internal clients such as product parts in the production process, data or analysis used by other organizational units, or prompt reactions that enable other parts of the organization to successfully undertake their part of the assignment.
- **Managing clients/the market.** Responsibility towards those who use, consume, and need the products and services in order to fulfil their needs or complete their part of the job; this refers to not only external but also internal clients and users from other organizational units.
- **Managing resources (finances).** Responsibility for the means, tools, raw materials, data, and finances essential for efficient processes and quality products and services.
- **Managing people.** Responsibility for the usage of tools, systems and processes for the sake of good quality

utilization (in the most positive sense of the word) of people and their resources.

Every manager can be assessed and his quality determined by measuring these categories.

Although managers may be good at undertaking these five basic responsibilities, this is no guarantee of their true and complete success, or rather, it does not make them superb managers. Top managers are those who, in addition to possessing the aforementioned qualities, can and know how to influence people, i.e. lead them—leadership. Here we arrive at one of the key relationships between these two terms: some people do a decent job in all their managerial roles and activities but are not good enough leaders and do not succeed in influencing others; some people are exceptional in their influence over others and are excellent leaders but do a shabby job when it comes to basic managerial activities. Top managers are those who are very good at both conducting key managerial responsibilities and activities, the craft of management—and at having influence over people they lead.

Unlike a manager, which is a formal and organizationally determined role (there are no informal managers), a leader can be informal. There are informal leaders who are not necessarily formal managers.

However, the two different terms of "leadership" and "management" have mutual, overlapping elements.

Figure1: The similarities and differences between leadership and management

Managers	Leaders
• Maintain • Plan • Ask "what" and "when" • Do things the right way • Structure	• Innovate • Inspire • Ask "how" and "why" • Do the right things • Strategize

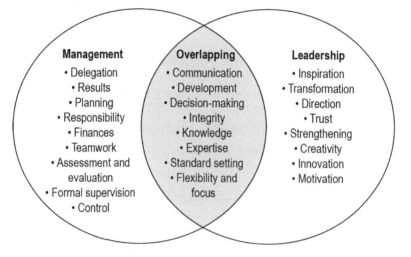

Some definitions of management position the terms "leadership" and "management" within the same space, i.e. in a way that does not differentiate between them, almost considering them as synonyms. Hence, one of the widely accepted definitions of management reads as follows: "the capability of achieving business results with and/or through people." Because of similarities and overlapping, there is often a misunderstanding of the differences between the two terms or even an understanding that leadership and management are synonyms for the same thing or same group of activities. Not only because of the foregoing, we are of the opinion that these are two different activities, positions, and terms.

Management is a formal role within an organization, while leadership is a skill or characteristic that is largely responsible for setting apart good and exceptional managers. That is, leadership is responsible for the crucial difference between managers who are exceptional and those who are not, regardless of the manager's level in the organization.

Perhaps the most illustrative way to explain the difference and dynamic of these two terms within an organization is the following:

> A manager gets or has subordinates.
>
> A leader creates or gains followers.

Although managers by definition get people who report directly to them and who report results and activities to them, their overall success and the success of the organization is not and cannot be optimal if their direct subordinates are not prone to following the person they answer to.

Within the framework of such defined differences in a socioeconomic sense, the manager is a more passive position to which the organization has given a group of people to manage, while the leader is a much more active position socially that, from the people he or she has been given to manage, creates people who are ready to follow him or her and do what the leader feels is necessary.

A managerial position, especially in very hierarchical organizations, also provides power. However, managerial power is formal and stems from position—a position that affords the possibility to reward or punish someone simply because they are lower in the hierarchy. And real power does not stem from position, but from so-called personal power, which consists of knowledge, authority, understanding, values, experience, and behavior—those elements that help you to influence people successfully, i.e. to be a better leader. Exceptional managers are also exceptional leaders, and they build their power on knowledge, experience, authority, credibility, and behavior. At the same time, they do not give up the power a managerial position brings, or the possibility to reward or punish, because they understand that this is also essential for successfully doing business. Bad managers do not build personal power (or know how to) but in principle only use their power of position—unfortunately, mainly through the power of punishment and not reward.

Thousands of studies on leadership have correlated business success and quality of leadership, regardless of the model or theory.

It is easily possible to find that individual elements of leadership successfully influence various indicators of business success within any organization.

Still, one assumption that has been proven innumerable times is that the success of any organization is always in high positive correlation with people's motivation and an appropriate organizational culture. In the next few chapters, we will therefore discuss the link between leadership and management on the one hand, and between motivation and organizational culture on the other.

Successful management and leadership are not possible without quality people, so we will link them to the processes of selecting and developing people.

Examples, Tools, and Research

Leadership and Trust

Figure 2: Leadership and Trust

Source: Phil Harkins, Powerful Conversations: How High Impact Leaders Communicate, McGraw-Hill, 1999.

The foundation of any leadership (even of quality management) is trust; it is only when people you intend to lead trust you that you will exert successful influence over them, i.e. leadership. Phil Harkins suggests a simple but powerful formula of trust based on the 4C principle. It is important to understand that there exists within the four elements an "and" and not an "or" relationship (to use an Internet search analogy). If even one of the four elements is missing, trust will not occur regardless of the strength and quality of the remaining three—and consequently neither will quality leadership.

Leadership issue of today

In a large study by Deloitte Consulting conducted in 94 countries in Q4 of 2013, covering 2,532 business and HR leaders, managers and specialists, leadership stood out as the highest priority in the area of human capital:

Leadership: Rated as "urgent" or "important" by 88 percent of high performers vs. 85 percent of average performers.

The executives in our 2014 global survey viewed leadership as the highest-priority issue of all the issues we asked them about, with 86 percent rating it "urgent" or "important."

Yet, despite the acknowledged importance of leadership, most companies feel they are not meeting the challenge:

- Only 13 percent of companies in the survey rate themselves "excellent" in providing leadership programs at all levels—new leaders, next-generation leaders, and senior leaders.
- 66 percent believe they are "weak" in their ability to develop millennial leaders, while only five percent rate themselves as "excellent."
- Over half (51 percent) have little confidence in their ability to maintain clear, consistent succession programs.
- Only eight percent believe they have "excellent" programs to build global skills and experiences.

At the same time, the same study pointed to the existence of the "overwhelmed/overloaded employee" and the significance of that element for the human capital agenda:

- Sixty-five percent of executives in the survey rated the "overwhelmed employee" an "urgent" or "important" trend, while 44 percent said that they are "not ready" to deal with it.

Source: Global Human Capital Trends 2014: Engaging the 21st-century workforce, Deloitte University Press, 2014.

Do these results perhaps indicate that organizations are generally lacking leadership, or do they show that the leadership is inappropriate and has thus far created a large number of overwhelmed people, a fact which it is currently unable to deal with?

Two

Motivating People

What kind of truth is it
When lie is on the other side
Values upside-down
Fear only fear

Dreams unachieved
You do what you do not like
But I can tell you
Where the road to happiness is—

Goran Bare, Majke, a Croatian rock band

Although seemingly pessimistic, these lyrics by Goran Bare from the band Majke are the opposite because they offer the road to happiness. But the road to happiness recognized in business circles through the increased motivation of people is anything but simple and not always optimistic. Successfully motivating people, amongst other things, means motivating them to do what the leader feels is essential or necessary. Followers are people the leader motivates into carrying out activities asked of them.

It is essential to conclude, not only through findings but also through common sense and intuition, that successful leadership surely implies a successful and quality influence over the motivation of those to be influenced. And a higher level of motivation, with the assumption that there exists at least basic knowledge, skill or experience, directly influences the ultimate work efficiency of every individual.

$$WE = M \times Ab$$

The work efficiency of any individual is a quality combination of motivation and ability.

- Ability encompasses knowledge, skill, experience, education, understanding, and knowing the wider context of the activity it is necessary to perform.
- Motivation is expressed through one's desire, will, self-confidence, faith in oneself, and presence or lack of fear.

This simple formula clearly indicates the importance of motivation for any ultimate realization, while the multiplication function tells us that even if the individual possesses all the necessary knowledge, skill and, even experience but lacks motivation (motivation is at 0), the ultimate efficiency of that individual will equal 0. Of course, the opposite also applies; motivation in itself is not enough for performing and successfully completing any given assignment.

Motivation in itself represents a very fluid and somewhat elusive concept for which no ultimate solution exists even within the field. Its elusiveness and instability in everyday work and attitudes towards people is clearly visible in situations in which an individual is motivated by something in the morning, while in the afternoon that same element will have no motivational effect.

For the purpose of avoiding very technical and complex definitions, we can define motivation at an operational level in the following way: Motivating people means bringing them to a position or state within which they are ready to exert additional effort.

Therefore, it is only when an individual has invested more energy and displayed additional effort that we can conclude we have succeeded in motivating him or her.

The ways in which we will evoke someone's willingness to invest additional effort are innumerable, varied, and sometimes difficult to explain. Still, there exist certain principles and repeatedly confirmed studies—basic technical concepts that have proven themselves even in practice and that we will simply recapitulate and elaborate.

Basic theoretical concepts

Although it is not our intention, as elsewhere in this book, to list and explain basic theoretical models, we feel it is justified at this point to present a clear overview of two theoretical models of motivation: those of Hertzberg and Maslow.

Hertzberg

If we begin with the set definition of motivation—the willingness to invest additional effort—we must also think in the opposite direction, of possible situations in which existing readiness to invest additional effort can be lowered or in some situations completely disappear.

Hertzberg's theory successfully explains both cases through a definition of what he calls hygiene factors and what are known as motivators.

Hygiene factors are elements, properties, and agents whose presence in itself will not lead people to a position from which they are ready to invest additional effort; however, their absence will lead to demotivation and an even lesser readiness to invest any effort or engagement.

Unlike hygiene factors, motivators are elements, properties, and agents whose presence in itself motivates people to invest additional effort and energy.

Table 1: Hygiene factors and motivators according to Hertzberg

Hygiene factors	Motivators
• Policies and procedures • Supervision • Work conditions • Interpersonal relations • Salary • Job security	• Recognizing a job well done • Development and growth • A challenging job • Realization • Increased responsibility • Success

Maslow

Maslow's model and concept of motivation is somewhat more complex and stems from the assumption of lower and higher levels of motivation or motivators; the higher ones cannot be met if the lower ones are not completely met first.

Maslow's hierarchy of needs or motivators is as follows:

5. Self-actualization: the need to work and to do a job we love and which fulfills us
4. Esteem: the need to be appreciated and respected by others
3. Social needs: the need for love and a feeling of belonging
2. Safety: the need to feel safe and protected
1. Physiological needs: the need for food, drink, sleep (i.e. basic requirements of life)

Table 2: Examples of organizational motivators grouped according to Maslow's hierarchy of needs and motivator

Maslow's Hierarchy	Examples of organizational motivators
Self-actualization	- Involvement in the planning of one's work - Opportunity for personal growth and development - A creative job
Esteem and recognition	- Reward as a result of recognizing the good work - Acknowledgement - Freedom to make decisions - An interesting and challenging job - Status symbols - The possibility of advancement
Social needs and a feeling of belonging	- Opportunity for interaction with others - Teamwork - Friendly associates
Safety	- Job security - Company security and stability - Appropriate supervision and control - Safe working conditions - Clear policies and procedures
Physiological needs	- Adequate salary - Regular and defined breaks - Secured and appropriate tools

Maslow's model provides answers for many motivational ambiguities or errors that can be found within a professional environment.

Primarily according to Maslow, meeting lower-level motivators leads us to seek out higher-level motivators that then become important to us. This means that, even if all elements of the first two hierarchies are fulfilled, people's motivation need not be high, otherwise they would then want to and seek to actively participate in teamwork, be acknowledged and rewarded, and participate in the creation of their work and responsibilities. *"Well, what do they want? They have regular and decent pay checks, good tools for the job, clearly defined procedures and they work in a secure company; what more could they want?"*

It is also possible to find managers and employers bewildered by the demotivation of their people, when they have included them in teamwork, given them freedom to make decisions and create; however, they forget or fail to notice that people are working almost without breaks, that they are not fulfilling all their agreed duties towards their people, and that perhaps the people feel they lack job security. In other words, motivators of a lower level are not realized.

In consideration and discussion of motivation, one can often stumble onto "high-level" discussions of how it is possible to awaken a higher level of motivation within people through various sophisticated tools such as relaxation rooms, creative rooms, flexible assignments and a flexible work schedule, a colorful and pleasant work environment, or working on fancy tasks and activities. Such an approach is unjustifiably over-discussed, over-considered, and is granted too much attention as it almost provokes a sense of spoiling by allowing only for the inclusion of a very small percentage of the total working population.

If we understand that the four largest employers in the world are the Pentagon (U.S. Department of Defense), the Chinese army, Wal-Mart and McDonald's, it is then necessary to think in a different way even if we disregard the military and focus only on the commercial companies.

The majority of people are today are those performing heavy physical labor (construction, mining) and repetitive tasks (processing industries, certain forms of sales, telemarketing). This includes many working in the retail industry at cash registers, merchandizers, assistant workers, many field salesman who have to attempt to sell the same product every day and sometimes even to the same client (insurance, FMCG industry), and drivers who follow the same route numerous times a day.

Elements of motivation for these people are not sufficiently discussed as they account for the largest percentage of people within organizations. Concepts such as relaxation rooms, a flexible work schedule, or flexible assignments cannot be applied to them because that would cause the entire organization to collapse. They have no time for creative rooms or creative activities, their physical environment is often defined by the weather, and it is impossible to secure comfortable physical conditions for them. Therefore, these are not tools we can use to motivate them.

Naturally, these tools do have a purpose and a positive effect in certain professional environments and activities such as R&D units, creative agencies, and high-risk and difficult jobs (e.g. air traffic controllers). But are these tools not exaggerated and overemphasized when we speak of the majority of people in their professional environments? Is it not a spoiled approach towards a significantly smaller number of people, which neglects the motivation of the majority in the business world and also all people within organizations?

First of all, the initial assumption of motivation for all people in a professional environment is, according to the Hertzberg model, that hygiene factors are met. In Maslow's model it is that first-level needs are put in order and fulfilled. Because of this, the first step, and one needed for any quality precondition for the motivation of people, is to order the hygiene factors, i.e. the first-level motivators:

- Provide normal, expected conditions for each work position
- Provide tools essential for completing the job
- Stick to all responsibilities that you, as an employer, assumed (vacations, rewards, overtime, benefits, breaks)
- Clearly define roles and responsibilities (descriptions of work positions and procedures)
- Pay salaries regularly and in accordance with regulations and agreements

A salary not regularly paid; bonuses not paid even though agreed targets have been met; working hours much longer than expected, agreed upon and regulated, and at whatever time the employer deems necessary; overtime worked but not paid for, despite the employer's contractual commitment to do so; regularly having to use a malfunctioning printer to print documents; a truck with a broken air-conditioning system; undefined procedures... These are all demotivators that negatively affect and are directly tied to work efficiency, which in these cases cannot and will not be optimal. To ask people to give of their best while at the same time not satisfying the expected conditions is, at best, hypocritical. Set and ordered hygiene factors and/or first-level motivators are essential although not in themselves sufficient to create an environment in which people will be motivated and willing enough to invest additional effort in their work and job.

With the assumption that all hygiene factors and low-level motivators are met, what are the elements that are truly motivational and bring people to a state in which they are ready to invest additional effort?

Hertzberg calls them motivators, while for Maslow they are higher-level motivators.

Following the satisfaction of hygiene factors and basic existential needs, the most important motivators are tied to feelings of recognition, acknowledgement, and belonging. There are a few exceptionally important ones.

Recognizing a job well done

This is a motivator which, according to Maslow, falls into the category of respect and esteem, but it is unfortunately very often in stark contrast to everyday practice—not only in the workplace, but also at home. It often happens that the good goes without saying, while the bad is recognized and emphasized. One basic psychological postulate reads: Behaviors that are recognized and rewarded have a much greater chance of being repeated than unwanted punished behaviors have a chance of not being repeated. The more a certain behavior or result is significantly recognized, the greater the probability and motive that the performance that led to results being recognized and rewarded will be repeated, probably leading to further success. The recognition must be real and honest, as only then will it have a motivational effect.

This motivator also has an especially powerful effect when leading a team, both at the level of the individual (so as to allow others to see which behaviors were positive) and of the entire team (so as to motivate all members to repeat the recognized positive behavior). In numerous studies this motivator was determined as the strongest in professional environments; nothing encourages additional investment of energy and effort like a good execution of this motivator. (source: McKinsey, "Motivating People: Getting Beyond Money", McKinsey Quarterly, McKinsey & Company, 2009.)

Good quality people want to be recognized, rewarded, and differentiated from those not good enough. A lack of recognition of the good, or giving the same recognition and reward to all irrespective of performance, is in fact not only to reward those who have fallen short, who have not fulfilled expectations or were the worst performers, but also to punish those who exceeded expectations. This is why such an approach demotivates them.

Communication

Communication should not just be an exchange of information but should provoke an experience: in other words, *how* something was said, not just *what* was said.

The importance of the non-verbal and the experience of information stems from our everyday experiences. Even the most unpleasant experiences can be mentioned in an appropriate manner, while the most pleasant things can be ruined and go disregarded if they are said in the wrong manner. Correctly said and communicated thoughts are once again related to high-level motivators and affect self-esteem and recognition, while also preserving a person's integrity.

Acknowledging invested effort without regard to results

Even the best individuals sometimes fail to deliver the requested result or fall short, but even a bad result might have required a huge number of people to invest effort. To punish them simply because of the result, while forgetting that it still required effort, has a very negative motivational effect on the person who will most probably have to repeat the activity that previously resulted in failure.

If the assignment was not done as agreed or planned, this certainly needs to be pointed out, but at the same time the person should be notified that the energy and effort they have invested, even for such a result, has not gone unrecognized. Recognizing the effort will have a significantly greater and more positive motivational effect on the repeated activity or assignment. This element, too, has a direct link to self-esteem and recognition.

Setting goals

People do not like assignments and goals whose realization is too simple or too easy, just as they do not like ones that are impossible to fulfil and realize. Assignments with the strongest motivational effect are those that are challenging and require the investment of additional energy, but are at the same time achievable.

Because of this, the process of setting assignments and goals is an art form that has repercussions not only on the financial side of the company, but first and foremost on the motivation of the people and the achievement of optimum results. Usually, the level of motivation for those assignments that "can be done with your eyes closed" and those for which "there is not a chance this can be done" is equal or very close to zero.

Therefore, when setting goals for your people, set them to be challenging but achievable and you will evoke the most positive motivational effect. In Maslow's model, this element is tied to esteem and recognition, and may be tied to the social motive if a team/organizational goal is in question.

A feeling of inclusion

People react very differently in situations in which their assignment is imposed and ordered without their being asked their say on the matter, compared to situations and assignments in whose creation they participated. The feeling of participating in an assignment's creation positively affects motivation and readiness for undertaking it. The lower they are in the organizational hierarchy, the less opportunity managers have to include people in such a way, but this does not mean they do not have any opportunities at all. This organizational motivator is tied to Maslow's categories of social needs, self-esteem and even self-actualization.

Purpose and context

We are *Homo sapiens*, a species with reason and a mind that thinks and for which it is therefore very important to explain, even for a routine assignment, its purpose and wider context— or rather, to allow people to take an attitude towards their work and allow for their work to have wider significance. A greater understanding of the context and purpose of an assignment positively impacts the motivational effects of the person involved in its completion, and is, according to Maslow, linked to self-esteem and, in part, self-actualization.

To these motivators it is sometimes possible, where it makes business sense, to add the more sophisticated previously mentioned forms of motivation such as relaxation rooms, creative rooms, a flexible work schedule or flexible assignments, as well as flexible benefits, individualized approaches, etc.

The significance of money for motivation

People work for money, expecting to fulfil through their work their existential and other needs. Looking through Hertzberg's prism, money is a hygiene factor, while according to Maslow it helps in solving first-level motivators by providing for one's basic needs. In the present system of values, it is essential.

However, in discussions with managers at all levels of the hierarchy, it is possible to observe their emphasis on, or better yet, overestimation of, the significance of money as a motivator. The actual influence of money and the size of one's salary can be summarized as follows. Salary, or money, has an exceptional importance for people's motivation. It carries perhaps even the most important influence in cases where the total sum of money made by individuals living in a community or family is not sufficient to cover basic life needs. This means that if the total income of an individual living alone or the total income of a family of a certain size is insufficient to cover basic life needs (food, shelter, clothes), then money assumes first place as a motivator.

This corresponds with Maslow's approach and the need to meet basic needs or lower-level needs/motivators. And if this element is not met, it is not possible to meet higher-level motivators. Rather, since salary also serves as a hygiene factor, if the minimal salary is not enough to fulfill basic life needs—without regard to the presence of other motivators—individuals can be exceptionally demotivated.

The minimal sum or amount of money necessary for fulfilling basic life needs is in high correlation with what is, in many countries, defined as a union basket (as opposed to a consumer basket). When the sum of the salary or joint income surpasses the amount of money necessary for fulfilling basic life needs, salary as a motivator significantly falls in the hierarchy of motivators' significance, while many other things/agents/motivators become more important. Then, although still tied to salary, two other elements become much more significant:

- A fair salary with a perceived correlation between the person's income and his or her invested effort and colleagues' income
- A variable salary that recognizes and rewards an achieved result.

When the total income is enough to fulfil basic life needs, the received salary's correlation with colleagues' perceived salaries becomes much more important. Perceived justice has a powerful influence on motivation. Consequently, many companies, especially those from countries where this is not a widespread business practice, would help themselves by explaining transparently to all their people the structure and manner of paying salaries as well as the math behind it.

Another important element when motivation and its link to money are concerned is a variable paycheck that recognizes and rewards results achieved. A transparent, well-defined, and fair variable salary that recognizes and rewards a good result is one of the best motivators. In its motivational structure, this is nothing more than a result recognized in a material manner, letting the person know his or her result has been acknowledged. As mentioned in the previous discussion, recognizing a job well done is the greatest and most significant motivator in an organization. The assumption of a good variable salary is an even better system of setting up and measuring professional goals and their realization, but many organizations do not have this aspect well developed and structured.

The fundamental influence of basic salary can also be described in the following way: By increasing basic pay, you will retain people for a while, but by increasing basic pay above the existential minimum, you will not evoke greater motivation or engagement in your people.

Money, especially when paid in the form of a basic salary that is the same each month without regard to a person's effort and work, does not encourage higher-level motivators and cannot provide for a sense of recognition, belonging, or self-realization.

As a possible conclusion about money, greater motivation can be evoked by:

- Paying a salary that covers minimal expenses essential for fulfilling basic life needs.
- Payment for all agreed extras, as incurred (for example, overtime).
- A payment system that precisely and fairly differentiates between the contributions of each position and its significance for doing business, with transparent explanation to all.
- A transparent and good variable salary system that recognizes and rewards the achieved results of each individual person.

CEO and "typical" worker compensation in the organization

Longer-term trends in CEO compensation:

- From 1978 to 2013, CEO compensation, inflation adjusted, increased 937 percent, a rise more than double stock market growth and substantially greater than the painfully slow 10.2 percent growth in a typical worker's compensation over the same period.

- The CEO-to-worker compensation ratio was 20-to-1 in 1965 and 29.9-to-1 in 1978, grew to 122.6-to-1 in 1995, peaked at 383.4-to-1 in 2000, and was 295.9-to-1 in 2013, far higher than it was in the 1960s, 1970s, 1980s, or 1990s.

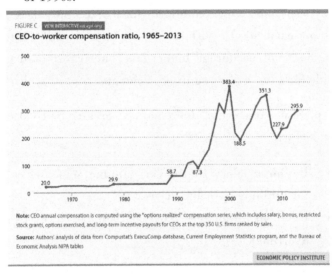

FIGURE C VIEW INTERACTIVE on epi.org
CEO-to-worker compensation ratio, 1965–2013

Note: CEO annual compensation is computed using the "options realized" compensation series, which includes salary, bonus, restricted stock grants, options exercised, and long-term incentive payouts for CEOs at the top 350 U.S. firms ranked by sales.

Source: Authors' analysis of data from Compustat's ExecuComp database, Current Employment Statistics program, and the Bureau of Economic Analysis NIPA tables

ECONOMIC POLICY INSTITUTE

- If Facebook, which we exclude from our data due to its outlier high compensation numbers, were included in the sample, average CEO pay was $24.8 million in 2013, and the CEO-to-worker compensation ratio was 510.7-to-1.

Source: Mishel, Lawrence and Davis, Alyssa, "CEO Pay Continues To Rise As Typical Workers Are Paid Less," EPI (Economic Policy Institute), 2014.

It is without doubt that the contribution of higher-ranked people is more significant for the overall success of the organization as well as for overall results. However, does the difference between CEO compensation and average compensation in the company reflect the difference in individual contributions? If so, what happened to cause the differential to increase from 20 to almost 300 between the 1960s and today?

Since one of the motivational effects of salary is the perceived fair relationship between an individual's compensation and the compensation of others, can this enormous difference between incomes be a possible generator of insufficient motivation?

The role of punishment

As mentioned earlier, the author's personal experience from numerous discussions about recognizing success and failure with managers at all organizational levels and their subordinates was shocking. In almost 100 percent of cases, when asked what happens in the company when a job is done well, the answer was "nothing." But, in all cases when asked about what happens when a job is not done well, the answer was that the employees were told immediately and without reserve. When the answers were not as extreme as this, an additional question was posed: In which case does the organization react more frequently —when something is done well or when something is done badly? The answers were, without exception, that failures, mishaps and bad decisions were more frequently and directly taken into account, i.e. punished.

Such answers indicate that organizations are considerably more focused on the bad, on mistakes and deviations, than on the good, so it can be assumed that they apply some sort of penalty more often than reward. A punishment does not have to be expressed only in monetary or physical form, but can also be written, oral, non-verbal, social (ignoring), or demonstrated in many other ways. This, of course, contradicts the already mentioned rule about human behavior, which states that desired behaviors will be induced much sooner through acknowledgment and reward than by punishing unwanted behaviors.

Punishment as a method is unjustifiably and unnecessarily often used in many organizations, which is why we do not wish to describe it in detail or justify it.

However, many managers do have problems imposing punishment even when it is necessary, well-deserved, anticipated and expected by everyone. Many managers either cannot or do not have the strength to punish clear and precise breaches of discipline, continuous and significant underachievement, or dramatic disruption of relations among colleagues or with clients. In such cases or moments of weakness, they have to understand the following principle:

- If we fail to punish those who clearly have to be punished, we actually punish everyone else. Moreover, if we do not punish those who deserve it, we are sending a message that such behavior is allowed and we are increasing the probability of such behavior occurring again.

A punishment, when it is clear and deserved, should be communicated individually, face to face, and very rarely and only in extreme situations in front of a group of people. Just like a reward, a punishment has to be soundly based, explained, and confirmed through examples of behavior and fact. The basic purpose of a punishment—just like a reward—should be a change in behavior, which is why the reasons for pronouncing a punishment and the behavior that caused it should be explained to people including the element of behavior that requires change so that the punishment does not need to be repeated or made more strict.

Leaders are the people prepared to take severe and unpopular measures, and punishment definitely falls into that category. Of course a good leader knows that he or she will get much more in return by recognizing good performance, and they will do it as often as possible and more frequently than punishing. They will not hesitate to punish someone if necessary, but they will not build their authority on punishment: they will clearly punish, while at the same time doing everything to maintain the integrity of the punished person.

Life-work balance, not work-life balance

First of all, it should be decided which of the two terms—life or work—is superior, more significant and primary. Without much thought, this is definitely life and not work, so we suggest a discussion about the concept of life-work balance, the balance of work in life, and not the balance of life in work. Often stated in the order of work-life balance, the concept carries a devil's seed by giving work precedence over life.

Management is sometimes—some people would say very often—not aware of the degree of burden on their people. To use a metaphor: managers will meticulously care about the total mileage on their executive car or request a replacement when mileage is in accordance with the prescribed procedures, will regularly and pedantically service it, put in the proper fuel, change the oil, change tires according to the season and so on. At the same time, they will not always understand that their allegedly most valuable resource needs servicing and rest' that a seven-day holiday is not sufficient for psychophysical restoration; that people cannot work for ten or more hours every day, including weekends; that people do not have a meter on them, nor an oil level indicator. But they do exhibit exhaustion, dissatisfaction, lack of motivation and illness, which in the end significantly reduce their overall efficiency. Normal working hours (which sometimes includes overtime), regular rest, shorter (weekly) and longer (annual) holidays are basic hygiene factors that, if not respected, may have a significant demotivating impact.

It seems that the imbalanced approach has been neglected for a long time, resulting in the fact that work has become everything, almost squeezing life out to such an extent that eight hours of work have become the exception rather than the rule. Every job certainly requires a certain amount of overtime, including occasional longer work hours and a greater engagement than usual, but if this becomes a rule, when it becomes "normal" to work for ten to twelve or even more hours a day, this yields ultimately negative consequences such as:

- Weariness and fatigue
- Exhaustion
- Frequent absence
- Illness
- Serious health problems.

Besides these physical and medical consequences, the psychological and motivational elements are equally important, if not even more important, for efficiency and business success:

- Dissatisfaction
- Lack of concentration

- Being torn between various life decisions
- Indifference
- Mental fatigue
- Stress.

The human is *Homo sapiens*, but he is also a complex being who not only sleeps, eats, and works but realizes him- or herself as a social being through interaction with other humans, through individual non-business-related activities that satisfy their individual needs and the need for self-actualization. If they have to work and only work, sooner or later they will experience saturation, fatigue, stress, and burnout, thus making it impossible for them to do their best at work or deliver the required results.

Are organizations prepared to pose one simple question and provide the answer to it? The question is this: Is the savings from having one person working ten to twelve hours rather than two people working eight hours each sufficient? Can they expect the final result of the ten to twelve hour person to be greater than the result of two people working eight hours?

On the other hand, if longer working hours are the rule and if most workers stay at work longer every day than formally expected, can it possibly be that the organization is poorly organized? If there is a constant need for longer working hours, it is impossible to imagine that all processes, working methods, methodologies, planning and resources are properly set up and utilized. In addition, a person who has no time to regenerate and has no outlet is dissatisfied or creates dissatisfaction among the people closest to them with his or her constant absence and cannot be focused or motivated enough to be oriented towards work. That person therefore cannot be efficient enough in the workplace.

The dynamics of the business environment and the everyday burden of working more than ten hours, and often more than six days a week, usually endanger one's private life in many ways besides overwork, stress, nervousness, and illness:

- Inability to attend a child's birthday because of an important evening presentation.
- Wedding anniversary coinciding with an urgent business trip.
- The weekend when one's closest relatives are coming to visit is disrupted with an unscheduled visit by the top managers from head office.
- The funeral of one's closest friend's father is missed because of an important and obligatory opening of a new outlet.
- A several-month-long assignment in another country just when the daughter is preparing to enroll in college.

In a motivational sense, the lack of life-work balance has a significant influence on people's motivation or, rather, demotivation. The security and proper organization of work should be such that, in most cases, work can be done within the eight-hour work period, and that is the primary role of a manager. And a leader's role and quality is in recognizing and understanding certain private human situations important to the person at that moment and enabling the person to attend to such situations. This will probably pay off in more ways than one through greater motivation, engagement and results.

The conclusion suggests itself:

The direct manager has the most significant and crucial role in the motivation of an employee. The direct manager has the basic managerial role and responsibility to ensure that all hygiene factors, or lower-ranked motivators according to Maslow, are satisfied:

- Basic rules, procedures, and work organization

- Technical and physical conditions of work

- Regular payment of basic salary

- Ensuring the fairness of the reward system

- Ensuring responsibility and clear business roles.

In order to get more, each manager also has to ensure real motivators—or, according to Maslow, higher-ranked motivators—by doing the following:

- Recognize the good much more often than the bad.

- Pay attention to *how* he or she communicates, not just *what* he or she communicates.

- Recognize effort, even in the case of poor results.

- Set demanding but attainable goals.

- Involve employees in the process of creating assignments, and not just demand the execution of assignments.

- Explain the context and purpose of assignments.

- Be prepared to make tough and unpopular decisions and even punish those who deserve it.

- Work actively with people on their personal development.

- Recognize important private needs and situations and enable people to experience them.

The more a manager exhibits such behaviors, the greater the motivation in his or her people, and he or she will have more success in influencing them and will present him- or herself as a successful leader. To conclude:

- A manager is a person who by the nature of his or her role and tasks has to provide the basis of motivation, hygiene factors and first-rank motivators through clear rules, procedures, systems, and processes.

- A leader is a person who, by his or her behavior and not by setting hygiene factors, brings out extra effort and energy in people behaving thus to meet motivators, i.e. higher-ranked motivators.

Neither organizations nor managers usually understand the power of true motivators—which are in fact the managers' direct behaviors—and they over-emphasize the importance of hygiene factors in the motivation of people, particularly those hygiene factors that arise from the organization itself. True motivators are nothing more than specific behaviors of the immediate superior, and no one and nothing else in the organization has a greater influence on the motivation of people than the behavior of their immediate superior towards them. "One comes to the company for the company itself, and one leaves the company because of the boss." The more the immediate superior uses motivators (i.e. specific behaviors supporting motivators) in his or her behavior, the more successful he or she will be in influencing people. In other words, he or she will display more leadership.

The highest demand, or curse, of motivation lies in the fact that hardly any manager or leader can say that they have motivated their employees "once and forever." Motivating people is just like gardening: you can never say that you have arranged your garden "once and forever." Neither can you say that you have motivated your workers forever. This is a continuous, sometimes painstaking but certainly not easily predictable, process; however, if you have done it properly, it is more than rewarding.

Examples, Tools, and Research

McKinsey's research

In its global research from 2009, which included 1,047 executives, managers, and people in non-managerial positions from various sectors, McKinsey established the importance of non-material motivators, primarily various behaviors of the immediate superior, and their greater importance to the motivation of people than financial motivators.

Companies around the world are cutting back their financial-incentive programs, but few have used other ways of inspiring talent. We think they should. Numerous studies (source: John Gibbons, *Employee Engagement: A Review of Current Research and Its Implications*, Conference Board, 2006) have concluded that for people with satisfactory salaries, some nonfinancial motivators are more effective than extra cash in building long-term employee engagement in most sectors, job functions, and business contexts. Many financial rewards mainly generate short-term boosts of energy, which can have damaging unintended consequences. Indeed, the economic crisis, with its imperative to reduce costs and to balance short- and long-term performance effectively, gives business leaders a great opportunity to reassess the combination of financial and nonfinancial incentives that will serve their companies best through and beyond the downturn.

More than a quarter of the respondents to the McKinsey survey were corporate directors or CEOs or other C-level executives. The sample represents all regions and most sectors. This underscores the opportunity. The respondents view three noncash motivators—praise from immediate managers, leadership attention (for example, one-on-one conversations), and a chance to lead projects or task forces—as no less or even more effective motivators than the three highest-rated financial incentives: cash bonuses, increased base pay, and stock or stock options (see exhibit). The survey's top three nonfinancial motivators play critical roles in making employees feel that their companies value them, take their well-being seriously, and strive to create opportunities for career growth. These themes recur constantly in most studies on ways to motivate and engage employees.

Exhibit

	Effectiveness, % of respondents answering "extremely" or "very effective"	Frequent use, % of respondents answering "always" or "most of the time"
Financial incentives		
Performance-based cash bonuses	60	68
Increase in base pay	52	71
Stock or stock options	37	24
Nonfinancial incentives		
Praise and commendation from immediate manager	67	63
Attention from leaders	63	41
Opportunities to lead projects or task forces	62	54

Source: McKinsey, "Motivating People: Getting Beyond Money", McKinsey Quarterly, McKinsey & Company, 2009

Tesco case study

On their website, but also in other ways, British multinational grocery and general merchandise retailer Tesco communicates to all people in the organization about the ways in which the Maslow and Hertzberg theories were integrated into everyday practice within the organization.

Maslow

Needs	What Tesco provides
Self-fulfilment	Tesco offers Personal Development Plans, recognition of skills and talents, opportunity for promotion and career progression programme. Career discussions feed into Tesco's Talent Planning meetings. The Options fast-track management programme provides a route for capable staff to reach higher levels.
Self-esteem	Tesco values emphasize self-respect and respect for others and praize for hard work, Its self-assessment, 360 degree feedback and appraisal system help to recognize individuals' contributions and importance and celebrate achievement.
Social needs	Tesco promotes team and group working at various levels; The company "Steering Wheel" assesses individual and group work and enables store staff to work as a team. Working conditions and a home-from-home ethos encourages long service.
Security needs	Tesco provides the security of formal contracts of employment as well as pension and sickness schemes and the option to join a union to give people a sense of belonging. It ensures health and safety in the workplace.
Basic/physical needs	This would include a place of work, regular monthly pay and essential facilities such as a restaurant or lockers for personal belongings.

Hertzberg

Tesco aims to motivate its employees both by paying attention to hygiene factors and by enabling satisfiers. For example, it motivates and empowers its employees by appropriate and timely communication, by delegating responsibility, and involving staff in decision making. It holds forums every year in which staff can be part of the discussions on pay increases. This shows recognition of the work Tesco people do and rewards them. Tesco staff can even influence what food gets listed on its restaurant menus. Employees thus become motivated to make choices that will increase their use of the restaurants.

Source: Motivational Theory in Practice at Tesco, www.tesco.com

Three

Our Behaviors,
Our (Organizational) Culture

Culture eats strategy for breakfast.

Peter Drucker, US management guru

Besides the motivation of employees, organizational culture is also an important consequence of leadership style and has a direct influence on the organization and its results.

According to a frequently quoted statement by one of the greatest theoreticians in the area of organization and business, the power of organizational culture is enormous, and so should be its meaning.

What is organizational culture, and why is it important?

Organizational culture is everything you can see in an organization. It is hard to define yet still definitely present. We know it is there; we can see it indirectly through the behaviors of all the people in the organization. Organizational culture answers the question of how we do things in the organization and how the job is done; it represents the organizational glue, the generator of the organization, and of the behaviors that exist within it; the reason people come to the organization and, more significantly, a reason people leave it; but also one of the most important informal reasons people in the organization are promoted.

Organizational culture represents a set of behaviors in the organization that make it a unique place to work. These behaviors are specific to the environment and what the people in the organization believe. Organizational culture cannot be copied, but you can notice it as soon as you enter any organization; you cannot duplicate it, but it is very obvious in any organization.

Organizational culture can be noticed through numerous examples, indicators, and situations:

- The way you are greeted or not greeted when you enter a company
- The way people address each other in the organization (by name or surname), especially in hierarchical relations
- Seating arrangement by floors, but also in offices
- Organization of working hours and free time
- Table arrangement in shared cafeterias
- Parking space arrangement
- Arrangement of the surrounding area
- The style of dress, facial expressions...

The organizational culture includes all behaviors that we can observe in an organization. That means that there is no organization without organizational culture—although there are organizations with no culture. Organizational culture does not necessarily include behaviors that are desirable in the organization or those advertised on gold-framed posters, but it is about behaviors that are actually happening in the organization and can be observed in reality.

So, why is culture important?

When organizations have a correct organizational culture, it has a high positive correlation with numerous (sometimes almost all) business indicators. When it comes to organizational culture, the key difference between more successful and less successful organizations is that successful ones manage their organizational culture, managing and guiding it in a desired and necessary direction, while in less successful organizations it happens spontaneously without control or management.

The organizational culture of successful organizations is in the function of vision, strategy, and strategic goals, and is built and managed so it can assist in their realization. In less successful organizations, the culture is accidental and unplanned; it is about forms of behavior that happen by themselves as a result of everyday dynamics and consequently are an end in themselves. As a result, the organizational culture in organizations can be divided into:

- Managed, directed organizational culture
- Spontaneous, accidental, unmanaged organizational culture.

Every organization has some kind of organizational culture, but unfortunately not all organizations manage their culture.

The Emergence and Structure of Organizational Culture

The following experiment with monkeys was attributed to Harry Harlow, a psychologist and professor at the University of Wisconsin-Madison, although it was never confirmed that the experiment was his or that it was actually conducted; it might be the result of someone's imagination. Still, its conclusions were applicable to everyday situations in organizations and the way organizational culture emerges.

In Harlow's experiment (which would not pass any ethics committee nowadays), five monkeys were put into a cage with a banana hanging high on a rope from the roof out of the monkeys' reach. The researcher then introduced a step ladder, enabling the monkeys to reach the banana. However, whenever one of the monkeys attempted to climb the ladder and reach for the banana, all the monkeys were sprayed with ice-cold water. After several attempts, they all learned the association between reaching for the banana and the collective punishment of being sprayed with freezing water. If they wanted to stay warm and dry, they should not go on the step ladder. From then on, none of the five monkeys tried to reach for the banana. There was no further need for the water treatment.

At this stage the researcher replaced one of the five monkeys with a new one. The new monkey, not aware of the icy water treatment, tried to reach for the banana. Within a fraction of a second, the other four monkeys pounced on him and beat him, again and again, until he stopped and did not try anymore. (Note that the icy water treatment was no longer being used.) The process was repeated, and another of the original four monkeys who had experienced the icy water treatment was replaced by a new one, and again all the monkeys beat the new monkey into submission. Finally, the cage contained five monkeys, none of whom none had experienced the icy water treatment. The researcher then introduced another (sixth) monkey to the cage. When this monkey tried to reach for the banana, all five of the others jumped on him and beat him. None of these monkeys knew about the collective punishment of icy water, and none knew why they were not allowed to get the banana, but somewhere along the line they learnt that reaching for the banana was not allowed. Nevertheless, none of these monkeys ever approached the steps to reach for the banana. Why not? Because, as far as they knew: "That's the way it's always been done around here." They had become the guardians of this rule without knowing its purpose.

The same happens in organizations. Any rule, regulation, or procedure is introduced for a reason. However, after a while the reason is forgotten but the rule, regulation, or procedure stays. Nobody knows why they are following it, but everyone does.

And that is how a company's culture is formed: Acceptable and unacceptable behaviors are initially established in response to important external events but, over time, all that remains are strongly held notions about what is and what isn't acceptable behavior. The origins of these beliefs disappear with the departure of the members of the group who were present when the patterns and standards were first set. In a long-established organization, there might be no remaining members who know why a given behavior is considered acceptable or unacceptable. Yet all members of the organization are quick to enforce whatever the cultural standards might be.

Sources: Adapted from Dr. Tuvia Melamed, Clearwater A&D, http://clearwater-uk.com/thought_leadership, and Fred Nickols, http://www.smartdraw.com.

Organizational culture emerges and survives on the basis of:

- Values and behaviors of the founder and initial management
- Socialization of the people coming to the organization
- Formal and informal rewarding and punishment of certain behaviors
- Nature and type of processes and procedures, especially initial ones.

Organizational culture does not answer the question *what* you are doing—the answer to that lies in your processes, procedures, systems, and products—but it answers the question *how* you are conducting work in the organization. This distinguishes you from your competition more than any other element. *What* you are doing is the same as what your competition is doing, but *how* you are doing it makes the key difference in relation to them. Both the *what* and the *how* arise from *why* you are doing it.

Figure 3: Organizational culture and success

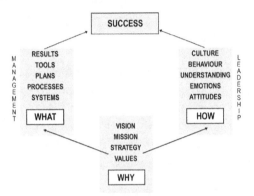

Based on: *Human Synergistics International,* and *Simon Sinek, Start With Why: How great leaders inspire everyone to take action, Portfolio, 2009.*

As can be seen from the overview, business success does not depend only on *what* you do; *how* you do it is equally important. Both arise from *why* you do it. This is why many organizations still do not achieve the expected results even though they invested their strength, energy, and time into changes and improvements of the system, plans, procedures, and processes. To achieve complete success, it is equally important—if not more so—to work on the development of *how* you perform work in an organization, work on attitudes, emotions and behaviors. In order to do that, one has to understand *why* they do something.

Successful management over organizational culture requires the understanding and management of values. And values are the basis and the prerequisite of any kind of behavior, or the answer to *why* in Simon Sinek's model. People have to understand *why* they do something and why they do it in a particular way, and the *why* is integrated within values, basic principles and levers of behavior. Values are the invisible part, both on the level of an individual and on the level of an organization that actuate and model behaviors.

He who has a why to live can bear almost any how.

Friedrich Nietzsche

In the famous and widely used 7S McKinsey model, values are arranged as a central element of a balanced organization and a key element for the development of other elements. It is impossible to replace or develop any of the other areas if the central part—shared values—is not developing.

Figure 4: 7S McKinsey (Tom Peters and Robert Waterman)

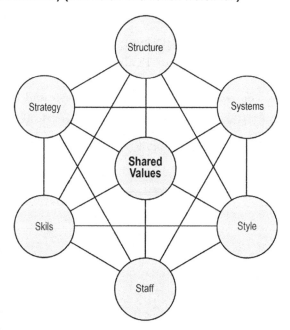

Values are not necessarily those nicely branded or drawn on gold-framed posters hanging on the office wall, but those that actually exist and have life within the organization. Many companies (especially multinationals) invest a lot of energy, on a declarative and formal level, in promotion and the branding of specific values that they believe exist in their organization. In reality, however, not only are those values non-existent, but everyday behavior is actually completely opposite to what is formally promoted. Organizational culture is not necessarily promoted through formal values but through what you actually live, and these two sides can be contrary and contradictory to one another.

The facing page contains a few examples of "counter-values," or a few counter-examples of declared values.

The mentioned examples show that culture is not what the people in the organization think it is. Organizational culture and its values are the ones truly lived and noticed in the organization, while the declared values are often annulled and "killed" by processes, systems, management style, and tools that require behaviors often opposite to those that should represent an example of desired values.

The values you would like to have, to cherish and live by, are the ones you dedicate yourself to, the ones you think about, and the ones you truly display through your behavior every day.

Table 3: Promoted values and the ways an organization "smothers" them

Declared value and promoted symbolism	Behaviour being a "killer" of a declared value	Possible behaviour supporting declared value
Innovation. An image and a poster with a radiant face and the inscription "EUREKA" above the head, or a poster with a word common for the organization, but written in another, polysemous way	Leadership and management style which requires completing a task without thinking or objection, absence of space for different opinion, intolerance to any form of different thinking or mistake arising from a different approach	Basic presupposition for innovation and its emergence in an organization is a leadership style which, as one of its basic characteristics, tolerates mistakes, especially those arising from a different way of thinking. If things happen according to how the boss says, there will be no innovation, no matter how hard we insist; anyway, innovation and creativity do not follow orders, but we may create a favourable environment which will stimulate them.
Client-centred. An image and a poster of a buyer who is leaving the organization with a broad smile, an image of two hands shaking, one of them highlighted and branded with colours and labels of the organization, and the other is recognized as the client's hand.	Parking spaces are marked so that the best and the closest ones are reserved exclusively for the management, so in this way we can track the hierarchy of the organization, while there are no parking spaces for the clients at all, neither in the area of the organization, nor nearby	If you want any value, to actually exist, including this one, in the organization and stimulate your organizational culture, you have to live it at every moment, at any workplace, any level of hierarchy and any behaviour. Therefore, the management would show that they were living this value by reserving the closest and the most attractive parking spaces for the clients, thus demonstrating that they too are implementing this value.
Teamwork. Posters showing sailing or rowing, or an image of a group of people from the organization with radiant faces after successfully completing a joint assignment	Individual Performance Management forms composed and completed so that all KPIs are exclusively and entirely individualized; thus, all employees are oriented towards themselves and their own achievement, and they are not interested in whether the organization was pushing them to think about others or about working with others.	Values have to be supported by the existing systems, processes and tools. Thus, in this case, the individual Performance Management forms would contain the so-called shared objectives, business objectives which can be realized and delivered only in cooperation and interaction with others; in that way, the desired value is systematically supported and wanted behaviours, in this case teamwork, are stimulated.
Trust/Integrity. An image or a poster of a person with eyes closed while another person guides him by the hand, or an image of a frightened client being hugged by a person from our organization, and then in the second image the client changes his/her expression into a relaxed and calm one	You are waiting for a client to pay an overdue invoice, and after a short while a contact person calls you very happily to inform you that the invoice will be paid tomorrow, you thank them and ask how they can be sure that the invoice will be paid tomorrow, and they proudly answer – "Well, there are already seven signatures on the invoice, and tomorrow there will be another one!". By putting a large number of signatures on every document and each and every invoice, we actually send a message that we do not trust one another.	In this case, the defined process and the procedure were the "murderers" of the declared value, so it is necessary to change the procedure which will support the declared value through required behaviours. It is sufficient if a few, two or three, lower-ranked persons sign some basic documents and some constant, current and smaller invoices, because even one signature should be enough to show and confirm that the organization really lives the value of trust.

The Power of Organizational Culture

Organizational culture, although hard to define but easy to notice, very powerfully affects many elements of the organization, its dynamics, and business results. Organizational culture correlates highly and positively with almost all business indicators.

The power of organizational culture exists and can be recognized in many details in the organization:

- Organizational culture has great power to drive away and expel those who do not act in accordance with it, regardless of their results. If you recall Ronaldinho, Eto and Ibrahimović, they were all fantastic performers even after leaving Guardiola's Barcelona; however, it seems that their behavior was not in accordance with the values of Barcelona's organizational culture at the time. Looking from the outside, the key values of Barcelona lie in some degree of modesty and keeping a low profile regardless of the player's celebrity, as well as orientation and dedication to the team, which was not always demonstrated by these three players.

- Organizational culture is one of the main reasons why some people are exceptional and achieve excellent results in one organization but seem to fail in another although doing the same or a very similar job.

- Organizational culture, or the behavior of an individual in accordance with the organizational culture, is often the more important (although informal and automatic) reason that some people are promoted within an organization based on the achieved results or estimated potential for the new position.

- Organizational culture and the individual sense of incompatibility and inability to fit within an organizational culture is, besides a negative relationship with the immediate superior, the most significant reason we begin to think about leaving a certain organization.

- Organizational culture, or the incompatibility of organizational cultures, is the most significant reason some of the greatest business mergers fail or have major problems in living and working together despite the size and power of the systems that attempted to merge into a new joint organization (examples are Daimler-Chrysler and AOL Time Warner).

The picture below shows the heads of AOL (Stephen M. Case) and Time Warner (Gerald M. Levin). Just judging by the picture, we can see that one of the two is rather formal (suit, blue shirt, tie, neat haircut), but he is obviously an extrovert, even a showman; the other is rather informal (suit and shirt in non-businesslike colors, without a tie and with a somewhat informal haircut), but at the same time, he keeps a low profile and is even a bit shy.

Their performances and descriptions are very different, if not opposite or conflicting; at the same time, they have the greatest influence on the creation of organizational cultures in each of these two companies. Is it not obvious that these two cultures were not only extremely different but also incompatible? After many tens of millions of dollars and a decade of attempts, this incompatibility proved an unbridgeable gap for successful joint operation and eventually led to one of the greatest-ever failures in business mergers.

Organizational Culture and Business Results

As has been mentioned many times, organizational culture highly and positively correlates with almost all indicators of business success. This is supported by many real examples from the business world:

- Southwest Airlines, at a time of great crisis in the aviation industry, had positive business results in terms of profitability, sales volume and increased market value (from 2003 to 2004) unlike the majority of its competition. Southwest is consistently named among the top five Most Admired Corporations in America in *Fortune* magazine's annual poll. One of the major reasons for its success is the organizational culture, being well-adjusted to business surroundings and synchronized with its vision, mission, and strategy. It was the first to introduce certain procedures and behaviors that changed the standards of the entire industry (e.g. the arrival of technicians in the cockpit). All of this was created by two CEOs: the first CEO and co-founder, Herb Kelleher, and current CEO, Gary C. Kelly.

- Daniel R. Denison, a professor from IMD, a top ranked business school from Switzerland, is one of the most productive researchers of organizational culture and its connection with business indicators. In numerous studies, he has established the existence of significant positive correlations among the four key dimensions of organizational culture according to his model (Adaptability, Mission, Involvement, Consistency) and various business indicators: Sales Growth, ROA(E), Profitability, Customer Satisfaction, Employee Satisfaction, Innovation.

Organizational Culture Management, Alteration and Maintenance

As has already been mentioned, when it comes to organizational culture management, there are two type of organization:

a) Those where organizational culture happens by itself (which unfortunately represent the majority)

b) Those that manage their own organizational culture.

Organizational culture management means ensuring that certain forms of behavior—considered as being in harmony with the defined strategy and which should facilitate and ensure the realization of the desired vision and mission—appear and evolve, and that they can be recognized and supported. At the same time, this means that the kinds of behavior not in line with the strategy, vision, and mission of the company, or which seem to disrupt it, are neutralized, reduced, and minimized. If necessary, organizational culture can be changed through several more or less drastic ways and approaches.

Replacement of the main person in charge

Although the most drastic, this is at the same time a very efficient way of changing organizational culture, which is generated from the top down. The higher a person is in the management hierarchy, the greater his or her influence on the creation of the existing organizational culture. This, of course, means that the person at the top of the pyramid has the greatest influence on the existing organizational culture. If this is assessed as unsustainable, or other business circumstances require a significant change of culture, very often the most efficient way is to replace the main person in charge. In this case, the issue is not that person's results (which can even be very positive) but the inappropriate and erroneous behaviors generated by him or her, i.e. an incorrect or inappropriate organizational culture. The behavior of that person is largely generated by his or her values, because of which:

a) The behavior itself is very difficult to change, i.e. it is necessary to intervene in a person's values in order to change the behavior, which is extremely difficult.

b) The values of the person at the top may conflict with the desired values in the company and be contradictory to them.

This change in organizational culture would be felt by all who worked in the company, in which nothing changed except the top manager, "Number One." The arrival of a new person would be recognized quickly through new values, attitudes and behavior, and the organization would become a different place to work, i.e. its organizational culture changes. The change, of course, may not only be positive; to ensure that it is as positive as possible requires two key preconditions:

a) To establish during the selection process that the values of the new Number One are in line with the desired organizational culture.

b) That the owners do not intervene in the management process; if they are significantly involved in everyday work and company management, the replacement of the formal CEO will not have any effect because in this case the owners are the ones generating and creating the organizational culture.

"Pulling in" and including other "quiet" people from the company

The existing culture in any organization is such, for the most part, because of the people in the organization who can be heard more, who are socially more present and more active—primarily those loudest by nature, the extroverts. Such a process does not evolve only in organizations, but in society in general; it is the "louder" people who build culture and atmosphere. Such culture is certainly not necessarily negative or wrong, but it may be. However, every company has a large number of quieter, shy people who are socially less present and less active—the introverts—but this does not necessarily make them worse. It may be that their values are in line with what you would like to evolve in the company, but their nature keeps them from becoming prominent.

Pull those people in—give them more opportunity to prove themselves and to manifest their values and behaviors, particularly if they are in sync with what you want to be lived in the company. You will be surprised by the change of organizational culture. However, be careful because by their nature the introverts are always a bit more reserved and they want to stay that way, so if you overexpose them socially, you may achieve the opposite effect.

In general, we live in a society mostly created by extroverts and with standards and principles created by the louder ones, while the introverts, for reasons unknown, are considered less worthy and less desirable. Just as there are very good extroverts who are excellent performers, there are equally worthy and good introverts. There are both good and bad performers in both groups. So, here again, the issue is not someone's result, but their behavior and influence on the organizational culture.

The selection of new and different people

It may be that the people in the organization have such a dominant value structure that they themselves cannot develop a change of organizational culture in the desired direction. We therefore use a method that enables a gradual and long-term change in organizational culture by selecting and introducing new people into the organization who we assume and believe have precisely those values and kinds of behavior we want in the organization in the long term. Here the issue is not the selection of new people based on their knowledge and other competencies, although this cannot be disregarded. Organizational culture may thus be changed very thoroughly and in the long run. In the implementing this method, the important thing is to achieve, as quickly as possible, a critical mass of those people with different, desired values. If that does not happen, the existing "old" people will be able to maintain the organizational culture the way it is and the desired change will not come about.

A change in the reward system and/or procedures and processes

People will continue to repeat the behaviors that are formally and informally rewarded or recognized, but they will also repeat the improper behaviors for which they were not punished. Certain behaviors in the organization emerge due to respecting or following the existing procedures, especially the rewards system.

A large number of companies are unaware that the organizational culture is what it is because of, among other things, the way the rewards system was defined. This means that the behaviors stimulated by the rewards system dominates, which does not necessarily imply that these behaviors are desirable. People do what they are rewarded for. If the rewards system is arranged around the totally personalized and individualized objectives of all those included in the system, it will result in greater interest by the people and they will pursue exclusively their own individual results. Furthermore, if there is open voting for the best employee on the basis only of the achieved individual results, you create an environment and a culture of competitiveness and mutual, even excessive, competition. If, at the same time, you only openly advocate and promote the values of the team and teamwork, the value in such a rewards system will be undermined and behaviors related to team and teamwork will not appear. In order to strengthen the desired value, you have to change the existing rewards system so that objectives are not exclusively individualized, but you can introduce so-called shared objectives whose realization is possible only if two or more sides cooperate. You can even change the bonus scheme if it is related exclusively to the results of an individual, so that a portion of the bonus depends on the achievement by the team or the organization as a whole, which will additionally stimulate behaviors directed towards others in the team.

If the desired value is trust, do not destroy this with procedures that require endless signatures and complete control because such procedures cause a kind of behavior completely opposite to what you want in your organization. When it comes to the value of trust, by insisting on ten signatures, as procedure demands, even on unimportant documents, we send a message one to another: "I do not trust you until you sign."

Pay attention to the extent to which your processes, procedures, and tools, especially the rewards system, are in accordance with the desired organizational culture and how much they stimulate or destroy the behaviors you desire for your organization.

Culture shock

Sometimes the change in organizational culture may be provoked with sudden and drastic actions, which aim to stimulate different behaviors. Just like every drastic action that seeks to provoke some kind of shock, such steps for the change of organizational culture carry a certain risk and may yield counter-effects.

The shock of the change of organizational culture may be provoked by redesigning the working area into an open-plan layout instead of enclosed small offices in order to stimulate greater mutual openness, cooperation, and/or belonging.

Alternatively, the shock may be provoked by taking away all managerial vehicles (which this author finds particularly attractive) with the goal of stimulating the organizational culture of equality, moderation, and so on.

Both of these steps, just like any other change in the organization, carry certain risks such as losing people not prepared for certain social relations and changes.

Systematically working on values

This represents the most thorough way of managing organizational culture; it is especially important during initial establishment of the organizational culture management system and defining values or in the case of a significant change in the system of values and change of the existing organizational culture. It requires substantial engagement, not only in terms of time but by everyone, especially the management, and it takes some time to feel the effects. This method has several key steps:

The selection and definition of key values

The first step of the top of the management pyramid—and in a way an exclusive assignment—is to establish the basic values, principles, and key levers of behavior that need to exist (or perhaps already exist) in the organization for it to successfully realize its strategic goals, vision, and mission. The principles of mutual action, as well as of external action, will ensure that the task matches the desired strategy and the principles that will ensure appropriate and proper behaviors. As these are key principles or values, they are usually limited in number, and practice shows that having three to seven key values in the organization is ideal.

After a responsible management has determined the key organizational values, it is necessary to cross-check their wishes and understanding with the impressions and understanding of others who are supposed to live those values every day. Organizations successful in organizational culture management verify the understanding of their values both with key clients and with their business partners.

After collecting feedback data from the people in the organization, all values should be defined so that they have a unique and clear meaning for everyone in the organization. Besides the unambiguous definition of values, it is necessary to define behaviors that represent the manifestation of the value itself, i.e. that they represent the presence and living of each of the values in the organization.

Branding

The eventually defined values are communicated to all people persistently, consistently, in various ways and at every opportunity, especially at the beginning or in case of a significant change. The most frequent way of communicating values within the organization is through branding with the help of special images, company colors, through posters on walls, screensavers, the use and publication of values through everyday means and tools, letterheads and other forms of communication with the outside world.

Recognition and reward

Systems for the recognition and reward of people should be defined and organized so they do not recognize or reward only the achieved results of the people in the organization, but also how much these people live and support the desired values every day by their behavior and example. This will be explained in detail in the next chapter.

Recognition of and fostering values and their importance may be supported by special organizational actions and events oriented towards their fostering, better understanding, and more powerful living. The activities depend on the courage and creativity of the responsible people. They could include a communal celebration and explanation of the rewards for the people who proved and supported the living of certain values by their behavior and actions.

Communication

As already mentioned, organizational culture management implies a constant, unambiguous, persistent, and consistent communication of values and behaviors. You cannot over-communicate in the implementation and management of values and organizational culture, so make use of every moment and method, although the most significant and most efficient is information coming from the top in a two-way conversation.

Recognition and evaluation of desired behaviors

Recognition and evaluation of desired behaviors is the most powerful and most efficient means of organizational culture management, whether changing and/or maintaining it. It is based on the already mentioned human behavior postulate: behaviors and activities you recognize and reward are more likely to reappear than punishment is likely to stop unwanted behaviors.

The basic principle of the rewards system that changes or maintains the organizational culture is that it contains within it the element of recognition and evaluation of desired behaviors and not just results delivered. In the process, the desired behaviors are not rewarded at all if planned and set objectives are not delivered, i.e. if the result is not achieved. Such a rewards system ensures not only the delivery of required results (*what*), but also the additional rewarding of the people whose behavior in the delivery of results was in accordance with the organization's desired culture (*how*).

Recognition of and reward for results is part of standard procedure for any form of performance management, and its realization is measured individually, i.e. by means of achieving KPI (key performance indicators). Recognition of and reward for behavior is possible in two ways:

- By a detailed description by those who proposed certain behaviors for which a person deserves to be recognized and rewarded
- By the evaluation of the nominated person by means of a questionnaire containing the behaviors that represent certain values.

Everyone in the organization may nominate candidates, but the top management should usually be the ones making the final decision, not the candidates themselves. Top management decides and explains why certain people were recognized and rewarded. The reward and the explanation should be public and well-known to everyone in the organization, emphasizing especially the behaviors demonstrated and rewarded. The system may have real pecuniary value but also other types of reward, and the rewarding may be done monthly, quarterly, or annually, depending mostly on the nature of the work and the size of the organization.

A well-organized system of this kind has a positive influence on the desired organizational culture in several ways:

- The desired behaviors as a manifestation of key values are additionally communicated to people, thus raising their awareness.

- It gives an opportunity to everyone in the organization to be active participants in the process by suggesting and nominating colleagues and also by being rewarded.

- It explains who the rewarded individuals are and why they are rewarded in a clear and transparent way.

- It motivates people to behave in a way recognized as desirable, so they themselves can be recognized and rewarded.

- It can, or even must, be a framework for all those who do not behave in accordance with the desired organizational culture, and this framework may show them the unsustainability and possible consequences of such behavior.

Organizational Culture Measurement

The most common practice in measurement or surveying of organizational culture, as well as all other forms of employee surveys (climate, satisfaction, engagement), is to invite the employees via a memo to participate in the survey and to collect data that are then analyzed by a select group of people. This is where the story often ends, i.e. other people in the organization do not get any feedback on the obtained results. In higher-quality environments, people are notified about the obtained results, but unfortunately environments that completely implement the so-called W methodology (from IRS, see below), i.e. that clearly define and implement actions in order to improve the desired organizational culture, are rare.

The purpose of organizational culture measurement is not the survey itself, but it does constitute a valid, legitimate, and goal-oriented activity for the improvement of corporate culture that should stem from the survey results.

It is important to bear in mind that once you have asked people to complete the survey, you have instantly raised their expectations that changes and improvements will occur in the surveyed area. If you fail to notify people of the results and follow-up activities after getting them to complete the survey and raising their expectations, you will end up with a worse situation and more dissatisfied people than if you had never asked them or demanded anything in the first place.

The so-called W methodology is therefore proposed for organizational culture measurement.

Figure 5: W-methodology of organizational culture measurement, monitoring and improvement

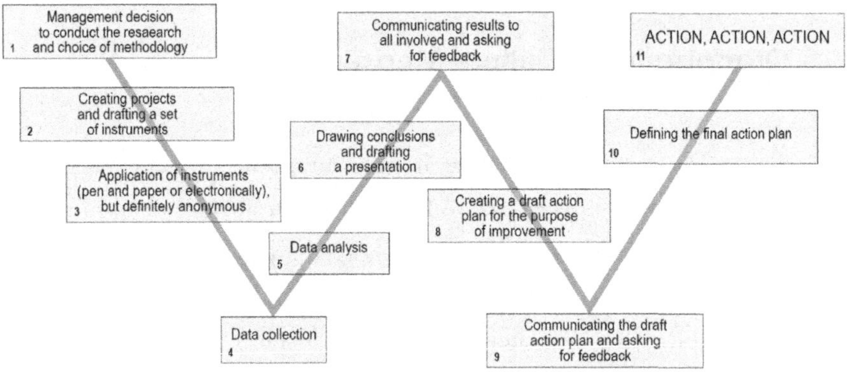

Adapted from IRS (International Research and Survey).

Organizational culture is identified through behavior; it is the result of all existing behaviors within the organization. Alteration of behavior is a demanding, long-term process on the individual level, and even more so on a group or organizational level, and the alteration of behavior often requires more time than expected. Surveys measuring and determining organizational culture should therefore not occur too frequently—certainly no more than once per year—and in bigger organizations even less frequently (every 18 to 24 months).

There are a number of highly sophisticated, expertly and scientifically confirmed and powerful tools and methodologies for measuring and determining organizational culture, of which the most well-known are: the Denison model, Human Synergistics, People Metrics, and Tower Watson (by IRS). Through their use and proper implementation, it is possible to determine many elements of the organizational culture, as well as examples and areas of room for improvement of the desired organizational culture.

Organizational culture survey analysis can be conducted on the level of various sub-groups in the organization to determine patterns and areas of improvement by thoroughly implementing the second "V" from the W methodology.

The key accountability for organizational culture and its measurement and improvement falls to organization management and the HR department, if there is one. They should be in charge of operational implementation and the coordination of activities related to organizational culture measurement, improvement, and management. As one of the safety switches of organizational culture measurement and improvement within the organization, the top management must also have in its KPI structure one (or more than one) directly involved in the measurement and improvement of the organizational culture; every manager should have one KPI that relates to the measurement and improvement of organizational culture within the unit of which he or she is in charge.

From everything stated about the organizational culture thus far, it is obvious that the key influence of formation, maintenance, and change in the organizational culture is, without exception, in the hands of individuals in management positions. The higher their rank, the more significant and crucial their influence becomes. Due to their influence on the existing or desired organizational culture, it is particularly significant to understand the role of line (immediate) managers in maintaining or changing the organizational culture.

The role of line manager as manager of the alteration and/or maintenance of the existing organizational culture is:

- To define, together with other managers, the desired organizational culture that ensures and supports fulfilment of the vision and mission.

- To define and regularly implement measurement of the existing organizational culture.

- To ensure that, in accordance with the obtained results, necessary activities are defined and implemented.

- To ensure that all other processes, systems, and tools within the organization are designed and implemented in a manner consistent with the desired organizational culture.

- To ensure awareness and inclusion of everyone in the organization through formal instruments (surveys, focus groups, regular meetings, targeted interviews).

- To define and implement systems that recognize the desired behaviors and to implement activities accordingly.

The role of the line manager as a leader in organizational culture is:

- To ensure that his or her behavior represents a model for all others within the organization and demonstrates and upholds the desired values.

- To promote and question the existing values, behaviors, and culture and their compliance with the organization's strategy, mission, and vision.

- To regularly and on a daily basis provide clear feedback on other people's behaviors and how these affect the desired organizational culture.

- To recognize (formally and informally) and reward individuals who support and maintain the desired organizational culture through their behavior.

- To clearly identify and, if necessary sanction, those individuals whose behaviors are not compliant with or jeopardize the desired organizational culture.

- To clearly communicate and use every opportunity to demonstrate the importance of behavioral and cultural values.

- To question his or her personal values and their consequent connection with the desired organizational culture, and seek feedback from others.

Examples, Tools, and Research

Kotter about organizational culture

John Kotter and James Haskett, Harvard Business School professors, published *Corporate Culture and Performance*, arguing that strong corporate cultures that facilitate adaptation to a changing world are associated with strong financial results. They found that those cultures highly value employees, customers, and owners and that those cultures encourage leadership from everyone in the firm. So if customer needs change, a firm's culture almost forces people to change their practices to meet the new needs. And anyone, not just a few people, is empowered to do just that.

One standout exhibit in that book highlights the difference in results over an eleven year period between twelve companies that did and twenty companies that did not have this sort of culture.

Exhibit

	Average Increase for Twelve Firms with Performance-Enhancing Cultures	Average Increase for Twenty Firms without Performance-Enhancing Cultures
Revenue Growth	682%	166%
Employment Growth	282%	36%
Stock Price Growth	901%	74%
Net Income Growth	756%	1%

These results are staggering. To consider that the difference between a nine hundred percent and a seventy-five percent appreciation in equity value is somewhat attributable to the strength of a company's corporate culture highlights the significance of this often-overlooked issue.

Sources: *John P Kotter and James L Haskett, Corporate Culture and Performance; Free Press, 1992, www.forbes.com.*

Apart from the data listed above, Kotter and Haskett outline a number of other examples of the connection between appropriate organizational culture and positive business outcomes.

The influence of the leader's personal values on organizational culture and the organization's results

The biggest and most significant influence on the creation of organizational culture comes from the individuals at the very top of the management pyramid, which means that the leaders of the organization have the greatest influence on the creation of organizational culture. Yair Berson, Shaul Oreg, and Taly Dvir tried to ascertain this assumption in the following paper.

The key hypotheses they set out were:

H1: Leader self-direction will be associated with an entrepreneurial organizational culture.

H2: Leader security values will be associated with a bureaucratic organizational culture.

H3: Leader benevolence will be associated with a supportive organizational culture.

H4: Members' perceptions of their organizational culture as entrepreneurially oriented will be associated with sales growth as indicated by financial reports.

H5: Perceptions of bureaucratic culture will be negatively associated with executives' assessment of the extent to which employees intend to turnover.

H6: Members' perceptions of their organizational culture as supportive will be negatively associated with turnover.

H7: Organizational culture will mediate the relationship between CEO values and organizational culture.

METHOD

Sample and Procedure

We contacted 139 Israeli publicly traded companies that represented both high- and low-tech organizations based on their level of investment in R&D. Data were obtained from 26 companies. To avoid common source bias, we used data from four sources: CEOs rated their personal values (N=26), direct reports of the senior vice presidents (N=185) rated organizational culture, senior Vice Presidents rated the ratio of expected turnover in the course of the year (N=71), and company sales growth was assessed from annual reports.

All CEOs, 82 percent of the senior VPs, and 69 percent of the reports of the senior VPs were men. Both the mean CEO age and the mean age of the entire managerial sample (i.e., CEOs, senior VPs, and the direct reports) were 44. The mean tenure of CEOs in their jobs was four years and their mean tenure in the organization was eight years. Mean job-tenure and organizational tenure for the entire managerial sample were 5.4 and 7.9 years respectively.

Measures

Personal Values. CEO values were measured with Schwartz's (1992) value inventory.

Sample items that compose the **self-direction value** include items such as "freedom," "creativity," and "independence." Items that compose the **security value** include: "order," "national safety," and "reciprocity." Items that compose the **benevolence value** include: "loyal," "honest," and "helpful." Value scales yielded satisfactory reliability (Alpha) coefficients.

Organizational culture. Ratings of organizational culture orientation were obtained using Wallach's (1983) measure that consists of three scales (entrepreneurial, supportive, and bureaucratic cultures) and a total of 24 items. The three-factor model was supported by confirmatory factor analysis. Scales yielded satisfactory reliability (Alpha) coefficients. Sample items for **entrepreneurial culture** are: "risk-taking," "creative," and "results-oriented"; for **bureaucratic culture**: "procedural" and "regulatory"; and for **supportive culture**: "encouraging" and "relationships-oriented." The Alpha coefficient for entrepreneurial culture was .78, for bureaucratic culture it was .74, and for supportive culture it was .85.

Organizational performance. While there is a disagreement about what constitutes entrepreneurial performance (Daily, McDougall, Covin, & Dalton), researchers tend to agree that such measures should reflect the temporal nature of entrepreneurial performance; for example, its emphasis on growth (Dess et al., 2003). Indeed, **sales growth** is considered as the "most important single indicator of entrepreneurial venture performance" (Ensley, Carland, & Carland, 2000, p. 68). In line with Shaw, Delery, and Gupta (1998), **turnover** in this study was evaluated via reports from key respondents in the organization. Based on Huselid's (1995) measure, we used a composite score on the basis of senior VPs' responses to the following three questions:

"What is your estimate of the average annual percentage of employees who voluntarily leave the organization?", "What is your estimate of the average annual percentage of employees who involuntarily leave the organization?", and "What is the likelihood that people in this organization will make an effort to find a new job in the course of this upcoming year?"

RESULTS AND DISCUSSION

Figure A demonstrates support for Hypotheses one through 6.

Mediation tests (Baron & Kenny, 1986) supported Hypothesis 7. For all three cultural dimensions, organizational culture partially mediated the relationships between CEO values and organizational performance. In other words, entrepreneurial culture mediated the relationship between CEO self-direction and company sales growth; bureaucratic culture mediated the relationship between CEO security and company turnover estimates; and supportive culture mediated the relationship between CEO benevolence and company turnover.

Figure A: PLS Structural Equations Modelling Results Picture from the source paper

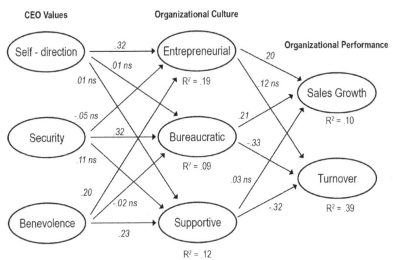

Note: All path coefficients are statistically significant at p <.001 level unless indicated otherwise (ns = not significant).

Source: Yair Berson, Shaul Oreg, Taly Dvir; Organizational Culture as a Mediator of CEO Values and Organizational Performance, Academy of Management Best Conference Paper, 2005.

Creation of a tailor-made or organization-specific set of instruments and tools for organizational culture measurement and management

Apart from the already mentioned powerful methodologies and tools available on the market for organizational culture analysis, it is also possible to create tailor-made instruments and tools. These, of course, are not a set of instruments with all the required qualities, nor are they necessarily tested and evaluated psychometrically and sociometrically with a necessary sample, but they can provide fairly high-quality indicators of the condition of organizational culture and behavior in your organization.

The steps for creating and implementing such a set of instruments are as follows:

1. Once you have a clearly defined organizational vision, mission, and strategy, work together as an expanded management to agree on and determine the key principles that must be present in the organization: the principles that will be upheld among yourselves but also demonstrated outwardly; behaviors that will support fulfilment of the strategy, vision, and mission. These principles form the foundation of desired behaviors, i.e. the desired organizational culture, and represent the desired values. Determine and agree on three to seven key values.

   Every one of the selected values should be described in the form of a simple, concise, and unambiguous sentence that will be communicated to the entire organization in an identical manner, and which should be understood in an identical or very similar way by everyone in the organization.

This expanded management group should also list related behaviors for each of the selected and defined values: those types and examples of specific behaviors that represent the manifestation and true implementation of selected values. Each value could and should be described with three to ten related behaviors, which should also be listed and described in the form of simple and unambiguous sentences that express the desired behaviors in a straightforward manner.

Example of a value:

- **APPRECIATION**: We honestly, tolerantly, and with an open mind, understand, respect, and accept the right to be different.

Related behaviors:

- We listen with understanding and interest.
- We respect everyone's values and dignity, regardless of their religion, culture, nationality, gender, or level in the organization.
- We provide the same opportunities for personal development, career development, progression, and learning to all people.
- We treat others as we want to be treated ourselves.
- We respect the contribution, time, knowledge, skills, and points of view of others.
- We provide and appreciate feedback.

This step may be operationally executed through two or three interactive facilitating workshops, each lasting one or two days.

2. Completely defined and described values and their related behaviors are to be communicated to everyone in the organization. Their feedback should be sought on the extent to which the values and behaviors are clear, unambiguous, and comprehensible. If your organization is small, you can communicate this to everyone; in larger organizations, execute this step through focus groups.

The basic purpose of this step is to verify understanding and the unambiguity of listed and defined values and their related behaviors. The aim is to ensure that the values and desired behaviors have identical or very similar meanings for all and are understood as such by everyone in the organization.

Collect feedback information from people in the organization and amend the original descriptions and definitions of values and behaviors as necessary in accordance with the feedback.

3. At this point you have selected and finally described and defined key values and described related behaviors. You also have the entire basis necessary for measurement and analysis of the desired organizational culture.

Since the organizational culture is generated from the top and since the very top of the management pyramid exerts the greatest influence on the creation and formation of organizational culture, it is necessary to determine to what extent their values and behaviors are in harmony with the desired ones.

Create a questionnaire using all the behaviors defined in Steps 1 and 2, in a manner allowing every member of top management to make a self-assessment of his or her behavior in comparison with the desired behaviors, but also in a way that allows people in the organization to make the same assessment of the individual (i.e. 360° methodology). It is desirable to arrange the questionnaire elements by randomly "distributing" particular behaviors from each of the values within the questionnaire instead of listing them in blocks describing a particular value.

Example of self-assessment elements:

- I listen with understanding and interest.
- I treat others as I want to be treated.
- I provide and appreciate feedback.

Examples of elements for 360° assessment by others (the heading should include the name and surname of the assessed individual):

- The individual listens with understanding and interest.
- The individual treats others as he or she wants to be treated.
- The individual provides and appreciates feedback.

Use the questionnaire, drafted as described above, to collect self-assessment and external assessment data. After collecting the data, each manager should receive feedback on the extent to which his or her behavior is in compliance with the behaviors they are expected to represent and uphold as the desired organizational culture, and to what extent they contribute to and develop the desired organizational culture by their own behaviors.

4. The key step in determining the current or zero organizational culture in relation to the desired one is to include the entire organization in the assessment of the presence of desired behaviors. Using the same statements/elements used in Step 3, create a tool that will allow everyone in the organization to assess the presence of each of the desired behaviors within it. The questionnaire should be written in first person plural, referring to the organization in its entirety (i.e. as "we").

Examples of statements for the assessment of the presence of behaviors in the entire organization are as for those listed as Related Behaviors at the end of step one.

The possible metrics used to assess the presence of each of the behaviors on an organizational level (but also on an individual level) are:

1. The behavior in question almost never occurs in the organization.
2. The behavior in question rarely occurs in the organization.
3. The behavior in question occasionally occurs in the organization.
4. The behavior in question often occurs in the organization.
5. The behavior in question is constantly present in the organization.

Results collected in this manner represent feedback from the entire organization about which of the listed desired behaviors are already present and to what extent, which ones are still not sufficiently present, as well as which values are already implemented within the organization and which ones are still not sufficiently recognized. Depending on how you draft the questionnaire, you can ascertain the differences in assessment of desired behaviors in relation to different groups of people within the organization (units, locations, hierarchy, length of employment, etc.). These results form the foundation for drafting an action plan that should be aimed at enhancing the organizational culture in the desired direction.

In accordance with the W methodology, it is of course necessary to familiarize everyone in the organization with the results of the survey, to ask for their feedback, to create an action plan, and to act in accordance with it. Do not forget to include SMART activities in the action plan and to ensure that the key actions form part of the KPI structures of responsible and key individuals.

The survey should be repeated after 12 to 18 months with an identical questionnaire to determine the progress made with regard to the desired organizational culture, by repeating Step 4.

It is also possible that, after a period of time, you will recognize the need to alter some values or behaviors, which must result in a change of tools, i.e. your tailor-made set of instruments.

Four

Attracting, Recruiting and Selecting the People for Us

During this module I realized how much time I spent in choosing my company car and how that amount of time significantly exceeded the time I spent choosing my closest business associate.

This is a quote from the paper by an EMBA student (owner of a successful private company) for the final exam in the HR & People Management module.

The above is a candid statement that fairly reflects a very common state of affairs in organizations.

When buying a new car, if they have the option of choice, managers will spend hours on website research, ask their secretaries to contact dealers and collect information, combine and configure additional equipment packages, make inquiries with friends and acquaintances, and altogether invest as much time as they need (probably a significant amount) in these activities.

When choosing their closest associates, they will not be as meticulous, to say the least, and they will certainly invest much less time but also much less emotional involvement than when choosing the managerial vehicle.

How much time do we dedicate to choosing the greatest value of the company? Do we understand the selection process and what it encompasses?

The process of employee selection and employment encompasses the following main steps:

1) Attracting candidates, and gathering information on them

2) Selecting candidates and choosing the future employee(s).

Attracting the Candidates—To Attract

Where are the people? Lack of people

When it comes to options for the selection and employment of new people, the experiences of many Human Resources directors, even managers in all functions and all levels of an organization, are fairly negative, at least in Europe.

Many industries, such as retail, hospitality and some IT and high-tech sectors, have a problem when it comes to filling vacancies and count themselves lucky if they are able to find an individual willing to do the job.

The majority of other industries, if not facing shortages of suitable candidates when filling job vacancies, face the difficulty (or rather impossibility) of choosing staff of sufficient expertise and quality. That the lack of staff in Europe is becoming or is already a problem is evident from research and projections provided for the Lisbon Council in 2007:

| In 2007 | 319 million working-age citizens in the EU |
| In 2050 | 274 million working-age citizens in the EU |

Source: *Lisbon Council Policy Brief: The European Human Capital Index: The Challenge of Central and Eastern Europe,* 2007.

The actual numbers and projections primarily indicate the problem of the physical lack of people, which will become particularly evident in the phase of new economic growth and increased consumption. These figures are cause for additional concern if we take into account that since 2008 a significant number of qualified and mostly young people have left Europe (and not only the "new" EU member states, but also the "old" ones) to live and work in other parts of the world. These indicators and projections can also be verified by a number of other similar data.

The fact is that the population (at least in Europe) is increasingly becoming older and that the number of older people is on the rise. As a result, in some ("old") European Union countries, the number of homes for the elderly has for the first time surpassed the number of kindergartens.

In Croatia, the number of pupils in elementary schools dropped from 384,634 in 2005 to 358,574 in 2009. (A similar trend is noted in most European countries.) This represents a huge loss of population for a country of 4.3 million people in such a short period.

Comparable data from other parts of the world confirm that this is almost exclusively a European problem, e.g. 60 percent of the inhabitants of Malaysia are aged under 30.

There are many cultural effects of this trend, and it is a well-known fact that in the UK, for example, the number of elementary schools where English is not the dominant language is increasing significantly.

A smaller pool of people and optimistically expected economic growth will result in a situation where future job candidates will have a significantly higher choice and their price on the market will be higher regardless of the job in question.

However, a more significant problem arises in respect of culture and managing personnel of different ethnic and cultural habits and behavior.

To be more specific, some EU member states, especially the new ones, will have to face a significant increase in non-domestic workforce that will necessarily have to be "imported" due to an insufficient number of working-age domestic workers. The basic, key consequence of this situation is the need to adjust to and manage different cultures with which some of European societies are not familiar. This places a new task in front of the managerial (but not only managerial) part of an organization when it comes to steering and building the desired organizational culture.

As articulated by Peter Brabeck-Letmathe, Chairman and former CEO of Nestlé: "Each top manager should speak at least two to three foreign languages," and not only because you will be working in multinational companies, but because your society will become multi-national.

Employee Value Proposition (EVP)

The possibility of choosing the employer and the position puts candidates, especially high-quality ones, into a position of choosing the organization that offers them more in all elements of their expectations and aspirations.

This is why the organizations need to change their approach to the labor market—where they, thus far, have appeared as the (rich) buyers—into a position of someone who is trying to successfully sell his organization to a desirable candidate.

Table 4: The employer as the buyer of personnel or seller of the organization

	Buyer's Market	Seller's Market
Employees	Costs, commodities	Investments, consumers
Supervisory skills	Optional	Essential
Hiring occurs when . . .	Positions become vacant	Talent becomes available
Fair treatment	Treating all employees the same	Treating talent differently
Poor performers	Tolerated	Managed out
Performance ratings	Tend towards sameness	Rigorously differentiated
Supervisory focus	Rescuing marginal performers	Developing talent
Organizational rewards	Distributed somewhat evenly	Distributed to talent

The change of this concept also significantly changes behavior towards the potential candidates. Thinking should not be limited only to what the organization can obtain or what the candidate is offering, but should primarily be focused on what the organization offers or what it can offer to a quality candidate to attract and keep him or her.

This is by no means limited only to the package value (salary, rewards, bonuses), but relates to the total offer of the company as a brand that the candidate wishes to purchase.

Imagine a job vacancy advertisement—not one issued by the employer, but by the ideal candidate.

Job position: Top expert in his area

Seeking: Working environment within which he can exercise his qualities and values, invest the necessary effort, and dedicate a part of his life.

The ideal organization must possess the following characteristics:
- Transparent environment of immediate and open communication
- Fair treatment of people within the organization
- Pleasant and encouraging working environment
- Appropriate leadership and personnel management style
- Reasonable workload
- Acceptance of the importance of the life-work balance
- Recognition of and reward for anything well done
- Active involvement in tasks and assignments
- Investment in employee development

The ideal candidate offers:
- Relevant business experience with success in previous working environments
- The highest educational qualifications in his area of expertise
- Specialist knowledge demonstrated in a number of projects
- Openness to different temperaments and characters
- Desire to invest all necessary effort in the successful performance of tasks
- Orientation towards the life-work balance

Organizations with bad reputations will not be considered.

Interested organizations must enclose a certificate of their eligibility as an employer, without any unfulfilled obligations towards the people in the organization or litigation with their employees.

Imagine a situation where the roles are reversed, a situation where the organizations do not buy the desirable candidates but are instead trying to sell themselves to the ideal candidates. It is a situation that does exist nowadays and will become even more prominent in the future, especially when it comes to high-quality candidates.

The organizations are no longer the buyers of workforce but sellers—selling themselves to the desirable workforce—and what they offer is embodied in the term Employee Value Proposition (EVP).

Figure 6: Composition of EVP through marketing approach

Organization + Position + Compensation + Organizational culture
Brend + Product + Price + Unique experience

Together, they must be arranged to ensure the life–work balance.

EVP is a combination of all the factors and elements that exist in the organization, making it a unique and desirable workplace for any (and especially high-quality) individual within and outside the organization.

Figure 7: Components of the Employee Value Proposition

EVP is a combination of all the factors/elements that exist in the organization, making it a unique and desirable workplace for any (and especially high-quality) individual within and outside the organization.

EVP is an implicit contract signed by both the organization and the individual, and it encompasses all the elements of the employment experience.

EVP is "the give and get" between the organization and the individual.

Some EVP elements are more tangible (e.g. package, position, processes, reputation), while others are less tangible and more difficult to reach in a straightforward manner (e.g. organizational culture, leadership style, communication, non-formal groups and structures, values). Some elements are more individual in their nature (e.g. package, individual values, organization experience), while others are of a more social nature (e.g. organizational processes and systems, reputation, leadership style).

In the age of massive and easy access to all sorts of information, it is impossible to hide or significantly alter real information about the image any employer forms to his potential candidates. The candidate has at his or her disposal readily available information about your organization that, only ten years ago, he or she had no way of obtaining or had to make a real effort to obtain only in part. In choosing a company and making a decision, the candidate will make inquiries and obtain this information.

The crucial elements for the candidate in his or her decision-making process about a future employer are not only the aforementioned solid elements of the package but also, perhaps even more so, the existing company leadership and their typical management style.

Once the EVP image is analyzed in more detail, we again reach the conclusion that line managers (i.e. total organization management and all their behaviors and activities) hold the key role in EVP formation.

When considering how to win over a quality candidate, the management must primarily consider the management style they implement on a daily basis and to what extent this will be attractive to candidates. What are the dominant elements of company culture and how much will the candidate be able to identify himself or herself with these? What are the routines and habits, characteristics and channels of communication within the organization? What type of emotion is predominant among the organization's existing personnel? And what type of working environment is that particular organization?

As in other managerial activities and responsibilities, the basic managerial rule applies here, too: in order to be able to manage something, it has to be measurable.

The most significant and most straightforward indicators of EVP quality are usually those generated by external independent specialized agencies. They use a specific methodology or research to include a number of companies within the same industry, geographical area, or business type, and measure employer desirability in two ways:

1. Employer's attractiveness for employment. The most commonly surveyed target group are young people who only need to get employment as trainees and who choose at which of the observed companies they would most like to find employment.

2.   Employer of choice and employer satisfaction. The same methodology is applied to a defined company sample (industry, geographical area, etc.), and their employees are asked to assess their satisfaction with their current employer in various categories. The categories may be extrinsic (working conditions, salary, benefits, and rewards), but also intrinsic (promotion and development possibilities, management style, life-work balance, job security, pride, brand marketing value, etc.).

Comparable indices are obtained through measurement and the implementation of a unique methodology, allowing employers to be ranked in accordance with EVP quality.

EVP quality can also be measured through indirect measures, which are usually used within companies and monitored as trends. Indicators that can also be labelled as EVP internal quality measures are numerous and diverse:

- Regular internal surveys of employee satisfaction
- Internal research of company culture
- Fluctuation and number of departures from the company
- Number of absences from work (sick leave, work-related injuries)
- Exit interviews
- Average number of job applications for a specific job vacancy
- Number of hits on the company's website, especially the employment section
- Number of likes on the company's Facebook page.

EVP is only as strong and as of high quality as its ability to "meet" the individual demands and needs of every individual person within the organization. The ideal EVP is completely individualized, which is almost always very difficult, sometimes impossible, and often there is no business need for such individualization.

A high-quality EVP is clearly segmented in relation to specific groups within the organization. Although some of you may have a negative view of segmentation, remember that high-quality individuals want to be recognized, to be differentiated, and to be treated differently. They want their qualities and contribution to the company's overall result to be recognized and valued in a way that ensures the majority of other people are aware. It is important and in the best interest of the organization to direct its activities, energy, and effort towards key people (those who contribute more) but without leaving out or neglecting others.

A simple method of EVP segmenting, i.e. segmentation of people within the organization, can be represented as follows:

Figure 8: Employee Value Proposition—Segmentation

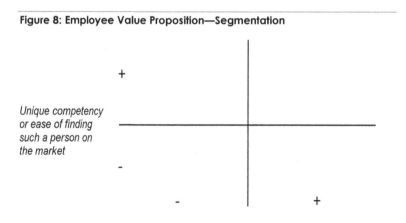

Contribution to the company's overall result

Naturally, each of the EVP elements can and should be defined differently for each established group, and EVP for every individual from a particular group can and must be created differently from the EVP for people from other groups. The simplest method of individualizing the EVP is to talk to your key people and determine and ensure certain elements of their EVP that will make them more motivated and keep them in the organization; these are usually not big demands, and it is easy for the organization to ensure they are met.

Employer Branding

In the present labor market, and even more so in the future, you have to construct your employer brand so that candidates can and wish to purchase it. Like any other brand, in essence it consists of the rational (visible, tangible, useful), but also the emotional (properties, relations, things, experiences). The latter is not always describable, but it is most often the reason we buy a product.

Employer branding is all activities the organization undertakes to construct a self-image of a desirable employer, and it is nothing more than the outward communication of your EVP. To be effective, these should be mutual activities of the HR function, marketing, and the entire management, along with all of the people. The higher the quality of your EVP and of its outward communication, the higher the quality of your employer brand.

The channels and language we use to address the people we would like to see in our organization are not all the same. Nowadays, communicating job vacancies through daily newspapers (which was common practice even recently), and especially through their physical paper versions, is almost a wasted investment, especially if you are targeting a younger, highly educated population of potential candidates. They do not read print newspapers and do not often buy magazines; that is something their grandparents do (though the latter may pass relevant information on, if they even recognize it).

The vast majority of candidates, especially among the younger population, seek possible employment almost exclusively via some form of electronic communication:

a) Internet editions of daily or specialized newspapers or magazines

b) Websites of recruitment companies

c) Websites of desirable companies and employers

d) Social media networks (such as Facebook, Twitter, LinkedIn)

e) Active participation in and use of various forums and blogs.

And while the first three of those communication channels do not fundamentally change the essence of communication, except in the technical sense, employers are placed in a particularly demanding position by the final two channels when it comes to attracting high-quality candidates. The problem is not whether the employer will open his Facebook, Twitter, or LinkedIn or visit the candidates' page on any of the social networks, but the fact that this manner of communication completely "opens up" and "bares" everything that the employer has to offer, completely revealing his EVP.

> I visited some forums and blogs and found complete information on [potential employers] and I must admit I was disappointed with regard to what I had read about them in the newspapers.
>
> A young financial manager's take on the new employer selection process.

In the process of selecting a new employer, candidates have more opportunities to find out information about the future employer than they ever had before—a trend that is likely to continue.

It is very important to emphasize that this is not (only) information of a formal nature but, more significantly, information that reveals the culture and atmosphere of the company. The aforementioned channels of communication allow for a greater exchange of information about the contentment/discontentment of people in the organization, leadership and management styles of senior managers, internal communication channels, fairness, treatment of personnel, and workload. In short, all the elements of EVP.

These are precisely the emotional pieces of information that are most important in reaching a final decision and choosing an employer. Employers should never ignore the fact (known in marketing) that out of ten people who are unhappy with a product or service, eight will share their disappointment with others, while only two out of ten content customers will share their positive experience with others. Candidates may not be aware of this rule when choosing a new employer, but they are more likely to be exposed to negative information about the future employer than positive.

All of this means that, as an employer, you are constructing your employer brand and communication quality not through the process of attracting and selecting candidates, but through everyday situations and activities with your existing current employees. The moment you embark on the process of attracting and selecting candidates, your employer brand is, for the most part, already formed and constructed. This situation can place you in a position where the candidates have better insight into some elements and occurrences at your organization than the people involved in the selection process.

It is very important to understand that EVP and employer branding are not only an external measure of quality, but also an internal one: it is not possible to develop EVP and employer branding outwards without simultaneously constructing an inward projection, image, and value. Indeed, EVP and, subsequently, employer branding should primarily be developed by turning the focus towards existing people and situations— then this image and information will spread outside the company.

Improving your brand image as an employer means improving your EVP, and this means developing and improving your organizational culture, leadership and management styles, processes, systems and tools, systems of reward and recognition, and attitude towards the people already in the organization. Only then will your EVP in the form of employer brand be communicated via the best and strongest channel of positive image propagation—your own people's word of mouth.

As already shown, EVP is crucially important in attracting and recruiting new people, but a high-quality EVP is equally important, if not more important, in retaining high-quality people (retention). A number of examples from practice and research show a high and positive correlation between EVP quality and an organization's ability to retain the high-quality people it wishes to keep.

Gathering Information about Job Candidates—To *Recruit*

Even though this part of the process may seem similar to communication channels towards potential candidates, which we have already described, it is significantly different. It concerns the possible ways of gathering information about those candidates who are of interest to the organization as well as the types of information that enable the organization to conduct a selection process of the utmost quality.

The channels through which we can collect data about candidates are numerous and varied:

- Newspapers and magazines
- Recruitment agencies
- Company websites ("Join us" or "Careers")
- Trade fairs
- Student traineeship
- Company employees (recommendations)
- University professors or secondary-school teachers
- Facebook, LinkedIn, Twitter

Even though selection, both final and as a process, comes after information gathering, it actually begins with attracting the right candidates. Hence the competencies required for a particular position need to be very clearly defined to help us determine the candidates' qualities and suitability for the organization and the position.

At each point during the selection of individual candidates and the consideration of their competencies, one should take into account that they need to conform to the organization's capabilities, i.e. they should arise from them in some way.

The key organizational capabilities a company has are the resources and abilities that constitute its competitive advantage over the competition. These are the basis upon which companies build their long-term strategies. The key organizational capabilities are the key characteristics, qualities and elements that an organization possesses, and which are at the same time necessary for the realization of the company's strategy and for its success in terms of market competition.

Dell considers a key organizational capability its distribution system, not its knowledge of computers. Coca-Cola's key organizational capability is the power of its supply chain, not its marketing power (although this is of course also important and supports the former). General Electric regards the following as its key organizational capabilities: executive resources (the ability to "produce" one's own resources in top positions), operational excellence (the "Six Sigma" process of quality management), mergers and acquisitions (the ability to take over and merge with other organizations), and finally e-commerce (expertize in the use of new technologies for commercial purposes). Johnson & Johnson has defined their key organizational capability as follows: "... company is not in the product business. (It) is in the knowledge business." The key organizational capabilities constitute the basis and framework for defining individual competencies and for establishing the individual qualities of the people we need in an organization.

The key organizational capabilities of Mourinho's Chelsea (strength and discipline), differed from Guardiola's Barcelona (combinatorics and creativity); therefore, to be a successful part of each of these soccer (football) teams, one should be a different player, even in terms of physical appearance. A championship-winning Chelsea was at least 100 kg heavier than a winning Barcelona team, and in both teams key organizational capabilities defined the framework of individual competencies as well.

Before you decide what kind of people and what qualities your organization needs, be sure to define clearly which key organizational capabilities your organization needs and how they would be successful in terms of market performance.

Sources of Information about the Candidates

Resume (CV)

The most common source of information about candidates is still their resume (also known as a "CV"), sent in response to classic advertisements for open positions published in newspapers, magazines, on specialized websites, or the website of the particular organization filling the position.

This type of information is almost always less detailed, relatively unreliable and often incomplete, particularly when it comes to strong and unchangeable capabilities.

On the other hand, this is the channel with which companies are most familiar; they have the most experience of it and know it best, which is why they rely on it the most and still use it more than others.

The most common mistake organizations usually make is that, after someone responds to an advertisement for a position on their website, they rarely respond to the person who has applied and almost never personalize the response.

Employment agencies

Employment agencies specialized in temporary and short-term recruitment, as well as headhunters, have become a daily part of business practice, particularly during the last 15 to 20 years. Such agencies recruit, either themselves or on behalf of other companies, candidates to perform the tasks required by the client company. These are mainly seasonal jobs, project positions, occasional business needs, etc.

Although candidates themselves do not necessarily have to be employed in the client company, they can be employed formally by the recruitment company or agency, although this puts the company in a contradictory position.

The negative aspect is that this way the company itself does not participate in the recruitment or selection of employees who would work for it (on the company's premises, with its human resources and clients). Hence it is possible that the required capabilities may not be exactly met, with the risk that the structure and quality of the desired organizational culture are being endangered or disrupted.

The positive aspect is that, besides the fact that this is the least expensive and most flexible recruitment option, it makes it possible to collect various and more than sufficient information about a particular candidate during a short-term employment—about his or her knowledge and skills and about the person's character, emotions, beliefs, and values—which makes any eventual selection likely to be more successful and of better quality.

Headhunters are companies that find potential candidates on behalf of a client company (mainly highly specialized and managerial positions). Based on a set of criteria, they find candidates who will be employed by the client. High-quality headhunters are usually able to offer very detailed information about a candidate and his or her capabilities and will narrow the selection down from a potentially quite extensive range to a smaller, targeted group of well-qualified potential candidates.

Besides the fact that their services are often quite costly in relation to other techniques of information gathering, a common disadvantage is they do not understand and are not familiar with all the elements of the organizational environment and culture where the candidate is to be employed.

Recommendations

In some circles, recommendations by people from the company, business partners, and university professors or secondary-school teachers are used quite extensively as a way of gathering information about the candidates, while in others it is regarded with a lot of reservations and even skepticism.

People of the organization, particularly if well-prepared and suitably trained, may easily recognize the way a person they know well might fit into the existing organizational culture. If they are of the same or similar profession, they may also be able to assess the professional qualities of the person they are recommending. External business partners and professors may not be able to identify how and to what extent the person would fit into the existing organizational culture, but they could reasonably assess the required professional capabilities of the recommended person.

If well controlled, these elements could turn into an exceptionally successful source of information about potential candidates. The negatives here are associated with the potential for nepotism, clientelism, and favoritism.

Facebook, Twitter, or LinkedIn

This is still a relatively rarely used technique for gathering information about potential candidates. But it is a great opportunity to collect the type of information we cannot access in the usual "official" way.

By exchanging Facebook profiles, we can obtain a lot more information about a candidate, about their values, interests, social elements, and even emotions, i.e. about all those elements into which we are unable to get an insight using the usual method of collecting information or about which we cannot obtain any details.

A more active approach is also possible by creating a Facebook group profile and by participating actively in discussions and exchanges of information with potential candidates.

This method puts the older population at something of a disadvantage, however, as this group is generally less experienced with these types of communication channels or may not use them at all.

Even though younger candidates are the predominant users of the latest communication channels and technologies, which can be used to gather information about candidates, it is both interesting and indicative that the candidates themselves who have a secondary-school diploma and/or a university degree prefer employers who are prepared to provide and exchange information directly:

a) At trade fairs
b) At open days
c) In an internship.

Source: "A barometer of HR trends and prospects 2011" CIPD, London, 2010.

The advantage of these information-gathering methods is the physical contact with potential candidates as well as the possibility for establishing two-way direct and on-the-spot communication between the interested parties.

The key quality of these three methods is the possibility for live contact between the organization and candidate, which improves and makes decision-making easier for both sides. Organizations should make the most of this, especially in the case of trade fairs, where activities unfortunately come down mainly to gathering basic information about potential candidates and the completion of application forms, whereas the possibility of two-way communication is what would mark your EVP and help you stand out from other organizations.

Open days give candidates an opportunity to feel (at least in part) the culture and atmosphere of the organization, which for many is what generates the elements necessary to make an emotional choice when it comes to choosing an employer. For employers, this is the easiest way to gather information about potential candidates. It also gives them the opportunity to assess, better than at trade fairs, the motivation and interest a candidate shows.

An internship is potentially an exceptionally useful and valuable opportunity for employers to get to know their potential candidates better, while candidates themselves consider it one of the most acceptable options.

In this situation, in addition to the requirements of the particular work position held by the candidate during the internship, he or she can familiarize himself or herself in detail with the culture, atmosphere, and dynamics of the organization in a direct way (through colleagues, the organization itself, processes, managerial style, form and dynamics of communication, reward systems, routine, symbols, etc.) and can also decide for himself or herself to what extent he or she fits or does not fit into such an environment. The employer, on the other hand, has an exceptional opportunity to assess the candidate in a direct way and to collect the type of information difficult or impossible to obtain during selection procedures (e.g. the candidate's beliefs, values, motivation, communication style, skills, knowledge, and emotionality).

An internship offers the opportunity to organize more extensive and numerous interviews, additional testing using psychometric tools, and detailed personal analysis containing information derived from a direct personal environment (the organizational units of colleagues and immediate supervisors with whom the person collaborates). Using a more systematic approach, the organization can obtain information indicating whether a person fits or does not fit into the particular working environment in a considerably more reliable way than in any other selection process. The disadvantage of this method is that it is not cost-effective (due to all employment costs as well as the person's actual stay in the organization), but even this potential cost is often less than the cost of recruiting the wrong person.

Selection of Candidates and Future Employees in the Organization—To *Select*

Selection begins even before the candidates enter the selecting process. It begins when the organization announces its need for a particular position to be filled (including, partly, by the choice of a communication channel), and it also takes place during the process of gathering information about candidates. But the selection process itself begins with the selection of candidates among those whose information we have previously gathered in any way possible.

The selection process is an activity that aims to minimize the probability of selecting the wrong person, or more positively, an activity that aims to maximize the probability of selecting the best/right person. A well-defined and well-conducted selection process significantly reduces the probability of choosing the wrong person, although it can never eliminate it.

Prior to any selection, and even before starting to gather information about candidates, a company should establish the precise criteria on the basis of which it will select its potential candidates. The necessary competencies needed to meet the requirements for a particular position in the respective work environment should be established.

Competencies are all the characteristics of a person working in or applying for a particular position that are necessary in order to successfully meet the requirements of that position as well as to fit successfully into the organizational culture and dynamics.

This definition provides two key elements or two main aims of professional competencies:

- Successful fulfilment of the requirements of a position.
- Fitting into the company's specific social environment, i.e. its organizational culture.

In today's extensive practice, the primary focus in the candidate selection process is on the first group of competencies for many reasons that to some extent have already been explained in our discussion regarding organizational culture. The second group is becoming increasingly significant and is more difficult (but still possible) to measure well.

Both aspects are of equal importance and should be devoted equal attention in the process of selecting future people.

The methods of establishing and measuring the first element have been sufficiently developed. But organizations pay a lot less attention to (and evaluate in a significantly less reliable way) the second equally important competencies element—fitting into the organizational culture and dynamics.

Why is this second element just as important as the first—if not more so? Has there ever been an occasion when you decided to change your employer of your own accord? Why did you do so? Do not think about the reasons related to your new employer but about what originally made you start thinking about changing and leaving your previous employer.

Practice shows that, according to a great number of cases and numerous studies, the following elements are the two most common answers:

- Not fitting into the organizational culture, and
- Disagreeing with the direct (line) manager (immediate superior).

These are the two key reasons why even the best people begin to consider changing their place of work.

No further analysis of these reasons is necessary to conclude that the deeper and real reasons for such a process are in fact different and distinct beliefs, emotions, types of behavior, and values and, to a lesser extent, lack of knowledge, experience, and education. Another possible reason for the significance of behavior, emotions, beliefs, and values lies in the following problem (not necessarily a final and unilateral response), which every manager at any organizational level has encountered in his or her experience:

Figure 9a: Who to choose, whom to thank?

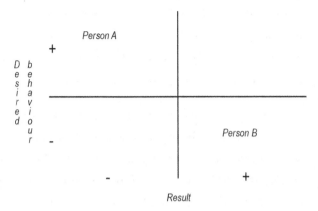

If, as a manager, you are required to fire either Person A or Person B, it is quite possible that your initial reaction would be Person A, but a more detailed and deeper consideration does not provide you with a simple unambiguous answer to the problem in question.

Person A underperforms—does not deliver the agreed and planned results—but their behavior serves as an example to all their colleagues and you wish all your employees behaved that way (e.g. the person supports colleagues in teamwork, communicates openly and in a clear manner, comes up with inventive solutions, respects other people's opinions, is on excellent terms with clients, and readily expresses opinions).

Person B, on the other hand, delivers the required and planned results in accordance with, or even significantly better than, expectations, but their behavior does not conform with what is required or expected from the employee (e.g. causes undesirable conflict, argues with clients, does not listen to the other party, does not look for ways of working differently and improving the work process). Fundamentally, the answer and the decision you would need to make is neither easy nor simple.

Figure 9b: Who to choose, whom to thank?

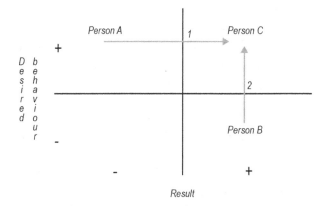

Result

There is something, though, that might make your decision easier: the ideal situation would be to hire Person C but, for that to happen, either Move 1 or Move 2 should be made. Practice shows that Move 1 is more probable, although not necessarily easier and simpler than Move 2.

All this indicates that, when selecting candidates, more attention must be paid to the elements that would define candidates' future behavior (values, beliefs, emotions) and how they would fit into the existing organizational culture than is actually the case in practice. Naturally, when doing so the competencies necessary to fulfil the requirements of positions (education, knowledge, experience, mental capacity, abilities, and skills) should not be neglected and should certainly be checked.

Just as, in the long run, you would not be satisfied with a person who has fitted into the organizational culture and climate from the beginning and has maintained excellent relations with clients and colleagues but lacks knowledge, skills, and abilities, you wouldn't be content with—or rather, you wouldn't be able to keep—a person who excels in knowledge, skills, and abilities but supports different values, beliefs, and behavior than those characteristic of the specific organizational culture.

In addition to the specified criteria and dimensions, when defining competencies in the selection process, special attention should be devoted to the question: to what extent are individual competencies subject to development, or do they represent the relatively strong and constant traits of a person?

When defining selection criteria and establishing the key competencies for the selection of future employees for your organization, special attention or greater weight in the final decision should be given to those competencies which are harder to change or develop.

The competencies that can be changed, or are easier to change or develop, are:

- Most skills
- Experience
- Knowledge
- Education and training.

The competencies that are harder to change, that is, harder to develop, are:

- Personality
- Mental ability
- Character
- Emotions
- Beliefs
- Values.

Of course, due to an urgent need and a tight deadline to deliver results, at times you would select a person who already possesses knowledge and skills, but you should take into account whether it is possible to easily develop this part further, rather than their attitude towards work and their intrinsic values and emotional structure.

Using a combination of these two dimensions—on the one hand dividing competencies into those necessary for the fulfilment of particular job requirements and those necessary for the person to fit into the specific organizational culture; and, on the other, capabilities subject to the possibility of development (and training)—one can conclude that the competencies falling into the category of main mental abilities, beliefs, values, and some personal traits would have an advantage and should be given greater weight when making the final decision in the selection of future employees.

Selection Techniques and Methods

The usual selection methods are:

a)   Resume (CV)
b)   Application forms
c)   Psychometric tests and questionnaires
d)   Interviews
e)   Assessment centers.

Resumes (CVs)

Resumes usually serve as only the first screening and/or first step when selecting candidates, although some organizations use this method almost to the exclusion of others.

Resumes can provide information about education and experience, and to some extent about knowledge and certain skills, but at times they only indicate a candidate's aspirations and value system.

The greatest quality a resume can have (and its contribution to the selection process should be) is to provide information about education and experience and confirmation of some existing types of knowledge and skills. Unfortunately, in terms of experience, resumes often do not offer the basic information required in selection, which lies not in where you have worked, or even what you have worked on, but rather what results you have achieved.

It is not important whether you have been a member of a soccer (football) team, even if the club has played regularly in the Champions League, but it matters how many times you were in the first 11, how many successful passes you have had, and how many times you have successfully defended or scored for you team. Being a player for a certain team does not mean much if you are following games from the substitutes' bench or are only called on to play during extra time.

This is why, when reading a resume, more attention should be devoted to the projects, activities, achievements, and results the candidate has accomplished rather than the evidence of or even excitement at seeing some of the candidate's previous employers.

One should bear in mind that resumes almost never provide information about candidates' beliefs, emotions, or sociability and only provide partial answers about their aspirations or value system.

Well-written and well-composed resumes are certainly one of the most useful selection tools, particularly as the first step in the process.

Application forms

Many companies create special application forms to be completed by candidates, asking them to provide their potential future employer with precisely defined information. Application forms can and should be created in such a way as to provide detailed and precise information about the desired range of competencies. They enable candidates to compare themselves in simpler ways, in terms of a set of criteria and required competencies. Even though they enable better quality responses, as well as collecting more precise information about education, experience, skills and knowledge (and even some information about their aspirations and values), this method is significantly restrictive in terms of information about personality, beliefs, emotions, and values. In relation to resumes, the advantage of application forms is that they provide more detailed and precise information about the targeted competencies. They can be designed to offer details about results and achievements rather than to serve simply as additional evidence of previous employers and positions.

Psychometric measuring (tests and questionnaires)

This method certainly belongs to the group of tools that can and should provide (more) reliable information and data, primarily information related to different intellectual abilities, personality, values, and emotions. Using this method, we can gather information about specified competencies in a very competent and professionally established way. Psychometric questionnaires and tests are one of the most well-known methods of gathering information about candidates, and they provide results of significantly better quality compared to other methods.

The difference between questionnaires and tests is that questionnaires are mainly composed in such a way that they do not offer correct or incorrect answers, there is no time limit to complete them, and many times they measure some personal trait. On the contrary, when completing tests there are strict time limits and it is known which answers are correct and which are incorrect. The main purpose of tests is to measure some of the cognitive, mental and intellectual abilities or skills of candidates.

Using a combination of questionnaires and tests, it is possible to obtain good-quality information about a candidate in terms of abilities and skills necessary to meet the requirements of a particular position, as well as information about the values, beliefs, emotions and personal traits that may serve as a good indicator and measurement of how successfully the candidate would fit into the existing organizational culture and dynamics.

Due to prejudice and excessive exposure to "quasi-instruments" from popular magazines and websites, there is often a negative effect or even a disparaging attitude towards psychometric instruments and their value as well as the quality of the results obtained. Psychometric tests and questionnaires are professional instruments that have undergone a long and complex process of pre-testing and preparation, all in order to satisfy two key criteria: validity (to measure what they are meant to), and reliability (to provide the same or very similar results in repeated measurements). The best-quality psychometric tests and questionnaires also require additional training and instructions for users and cannot usually be found free of charge on the Internet. Proper psychometric instruments exclude the use of "approximate" or "rule of thumb" methods.

There are several possible disadvantages to the use of psychometric methods:

- There are a huge number of tests and questionnaires for all types of capabilities on the market and in widespread use. Of course, not all of them are of sufficient quality in terms of psychometric indicators, and various versions of the same instruments can differ greatly in terms of the final result they provide. This is why it is necessary (and in some countries stipulated by law) that this method is chosen, used, analyzed, and, particularly, interpreted by persons trained to do so and who have the necessary qualifications; these experts are mainly psychologists.

- This method is very widely used, sometimes even uncritically, so the next potential problem is related to the use of psychological questionnaires and candidate "retraining" tests. Excessive use leads to candidates becoming familiar with the completion of these instruments, at times even to the extent of knowing of the correct and incorrect (or desired and undesired) answers.

- Questionnaires and tests do not offer the possibility of "live contact and experience" with the candidate. Direct contact with the candidate, along with all its restrictions and disadvantages, offers an important interactive element for the final decision in candidate selection.

Interviews

This is by far the widest and most extensively used selection method. It is a method experienced by almost everyone during their lives, often more than once, when being employed by almost any employer, but also a method that every manager, especially at middle or high organizational level, has used at least once to employ a candidate.

Although the interview is the most commonly used method, its professional statistical indicators in terms of quality when selecting a candidate do not place it above other methods. Moreover, its prediction validity, i.e. its ability to assess and establish a candidate's quality in the future, has been given a very low mark.

The explanation for its disadvantages and weaknesses may be considered in the following definition:

The selection interview is a reciprocal sales process.

This is a process in which the organization is trying to sell itself to a (good-quality) candidate, and in which the candidate in turn is also trying to sell himself or herself to the (desired) organization. At the same time, the selling process, as all who have experience in sales know, is an activity in which one tries to hide one's weaknesses and faults by any means available, and certainly to emphasize and highlight their personal strengths and qualities. This is a two-way process during the interview that is not always intentional.

The greatest advantage of the interview is the live contact and interaction with the candidate, as well as the actual experience, which should certainly be taken into as part of the selection process (although not the only one, or the most important).

The quality of an interview can be improved in many ways:

- It is essential to train future assessors on how to conduct a selection interview. The interview is a skill with its own rules, laws, structure, and purpose, so special skills are necessary to use it successfully, among which listening and questioning skills are of key importance. Quite often, it is considered that a good-quality interview can be carried out by anyone, with the result that interviews are often conducted by people who have not been trained for the task at all.

- Clearly defining the required competencies to be assessed during the selection interview. This helps to focus the conversation on the defined criteria and to ensure it resembles a casual introduction over coffee as little as possible.

- Where two or more interviewers participate in the interview, it is essential to establish clearly each person's role and the questions each will ask, both with regard to what competencies should be addressed and to which of them more time should be devoted. Unfortunately, practice often shows that the interviewers are "competing" in front of the candidate in their attempts to show who is the more important figure and the better performer in this situation.

- If a candidate is invited to several interviews, make sure you are not asking the same questions and requesting the same information, thus making the interviews seem alike. This risks leaving the candidate with the impression that there is insufficient interpersonal or inter-organizational communication in your company.

- When using the interview method, the best results for the selection process can be achieved by conducting a well-structured interview, with clearly defined assessment criteria and questions that help carry on the conversation in terms of each capability separately as well as defining the way in which each competency should be evaluated and assessed. This should be taken into consideration particularly when the interview is conducted by several (but not too many) trained interviewers.

- When conducting a selection interview, also make sure to:
    - Inform the candidates with sufficient notice about when the interview will take place and how long it will last.
    - Provide premises where the interview can take place without any distractions.
    - Inform all relevant people from the organization (e.g. at reception) that the interview will be taking place.
    - Take notes with clear observations but without interpretation.
    - Prepare the candidate's evaluation, in the previously agreed way, immediately after the interview has been conducted.
    - Compare all candidates according to the agreed criteria as soon as possible after all interviews have been concluded.

These may appear small and unimportant technical details, but they do matter.

The greatest and most irreplaceable advantage of the interview in relation to other selection methods is the live contact, experience, and intuition, which should always be taken into consideration when selecting a candidate. In this light, if well conducted, an interview can provide you with very useful information about how the candidate would adapt to and fit into the existing organizational culture and dynamics. It could also give quite good indications about their emotions, beliefs, and values.

Assessment Centers

This is one of the most reliable and best-quality methods when selecting a candidate for a position. It is effective and powerful when selecting a candidate in terms of both key criteria: the ability to fulfil the requirements of a certain position and the ability to fit into the existing organizational culture.

The assessment center combines several different techniques and instruments to assess the probability of a candidate's success in the future on the basis of combined achieved results. When assessing a candidate, the assessment center uses the following instruments and techniques:

- Psychometric questionnaires and tests
- Interviews
- Monitoring performance in problem-solving, teamwork and social situations
- Presentations
- Real-life scenarios (role-play).

Assessment centers are generally conducted by professional and trained personnel qualified to use this method; however, in order to obtain more valid and reliable data during the selection process, experts in certain business areas may also be involved.

The main principle of the assessment center is that each candidate should be assessed in each of the assessed situations by several qualified people using identical, previously defined criteria and assessment methods.

The assessment center is an excellent tool in the selection process, and in relation to other methods and instruments it has greater validity in predicting future performance, the candidate's successful fulfilment of the requirements of a future position, and how he or she would fit into the existing organizational culture.

The disadvantages of this method are that it takes longer than other options, is very difficult and demanding when used extensively upon a larger number of candidates, needs to be firmly conducted by specially-trained individuals, and is significantly more expensive than other selection methods.

The quality indicators of the recruitment and selection process may be direct—e.g. the number of people who have left or have had to leave the organization, especially early in the recruitment phase—or indirect, among which the most powerful is of course the final result. Good-quality selection and recruitment is impossible without the direct and active involvement of the immediate supervisor, i.e. once again the activities and behavior that would be undertaken by the immediate supervisor in his or her capacity as a manager and leader.

The immediate supervisor as a manager should do the following:

- Ensures instruments, systems and processes that strengthen the EVP.

- Ensures internal and external EVP communication.

- Plans the need for people in his or her organization or unit.

- Communicates the need for more people early on to the employees who need to be involved in the process.

- Communicates the competencies that should be required of the new employee.

- Is trained for the selection process, especially to conduct a selection interview.

- Participates in all selection steps professionally, representing the organization.

- Insists upon and ensures high-quality communication with all candidates.

- Ensures the availability of time and space for uninterrupted selection activities, particularly the selection interview.

- When deciding upon the selection, he or she is guided by previously defined criteria (competencies).

- Collaborates with the HR representative, if there is such a position, so as to ensure the best-possible selection process.

The immediate supervisor as a leader in the selection process should also do the following:

- Through his or her own behavior and leadership and management style, strengthens the organization's EVP.

- Encourages all people within the organization to communicate the EVP elements, both within the organization and externally.

- Insists upon the selection (at times even on the recruitment) of a good-quality candidate to whom he or she has been introduced in any way, regardless of whether at that point there exists a formal position into which a good-quality potential employee could be hired.

- Expresses opinions about candidates independently but openly and listens to and accepts with understanding the marks and assessments made by all others involved in the selection process when assessing a candidate.

- Recognizes and hires persons who are unlike or even better than himself or herself.

- Insists upon the recognition and use of all necessary criteria, particularly of those related to the existing or desired organizational culture (values, beliefs, emotions).

- Admits his or her mistake in the event of selecting unsuitable people and analyzes the reasons the mistake occurred.

Examples, Tools, and Research

The Towers Watson Study

Substantial problems in attracting and finding suitable new people, as well as EVP's importance and power in attracting and retaining high-quality employees, were established in a large-scale study conducted by Towers Watson in 2012 (1,605 survey respondents from all over the world and from various industries).

Key Findings

Attraction

- Almost three-quarters of survey respondents (72 percent) cite problems attracting critical-skill employees.
- About six in ten have difficulty attracting high potential and top-performing workers (60 percent and 59 percent, respectively).
- In addition, 43 percent have problems attracting diverse employee populations.

Retention

- Almost six in ten companies report difficulty retaining critical-skill employees; similar proportions have difficulty retaining high-potential employees and top performers.
- More than four in ten respondents also cite issues retaining employees with tenures of 18 months to three years.

Sustainable Engagement

- Employers that have segmented the workforce and deliver customized EVPs for critical employee segments are more than four times as likely to report that their employees are highly engaged than organizations with more tactical, less integrated EVPs.

- More than three times as many employees (58 percent versus 16 percent) are highly engaged at companies that have highly effective EVPs than at companies with low EVP effectiveness.

Segmentation and Differentiation

- Only 18 percent of the survey respondents have differentiated their EVP from other organizations with whom they compete for talent.

- Organizations that have segmented the workforce and that deliver customized EVPs for critical employee segments are nearly twice as likely as companies with more tactical and less integrated EVPs (27.6 percent versus 14.5 percent, respectively) to report financial performance substantially above their peer group.

Measurement and Monitoring

- Organizations with a highly effective EVP are more than twice as likely to capture external benchmarking data on talent management programs, and about 60 percent more likely to examine trends in total rewards program design, than companies with less developed or poorly executed EVPs. They are also about 60 percent more likely to assess business performance and conduct other analytics to review total rewards programs.

- Eight in ten organizations with highly effective EVPs regularly monitor the effectiveness of most of their programs, far above the rate of other organizations.

Source: *The Next High-Stakes Quest, Balancing Employer and Employee Priorities 2012-2013, Global Talent Management and Rewards Study*, Towers Watson, 2012.

The Universum Study

The study conducted by Universum in 2009, which included almost 300 universities and business schools in the U.S.A. with approximately 70,000 students, established the expected changes in terms of preferences when choosing a job and an employer. It also took into consideration awareness of the financial crisis that year, which increased demand for job security and financially strong employers, less demand when choosing job characteristics, decreasing attraction of the financial industry, lower expected salaries.

CATEGORY	ELEMENT	2008 – 2009 diff
Security	Job security	11.20% ↑
	Financially strong employer	5.63% ↑
Job characteristics	Challenging work	7.01% ↓
	Variety of tasks/assignments	4.73% ↓
	Being intellectually challenged	5.73% ↓
Work–life balance	Control over work hours	4.98% ↑
	Flexible working conditions	3.58% ↑
Industry	Financial services	the biggest drop
Salary	After 5 yrs ($75,000–$50,000)	significantly less
	Competitive salary	remains strong
	Performance-related bonuses	5.00% ↑

Source: *Universum MTU Presentation, "Employer Branding and What to do in a Time of Recession," Universum*, 2009, www.universumglobal.com.

However, in spite of the crisis awareness and the specified changes in job and employer preferences, the life-work balance has become even more important for the respective population segment.

Methods of selection—prediction validity

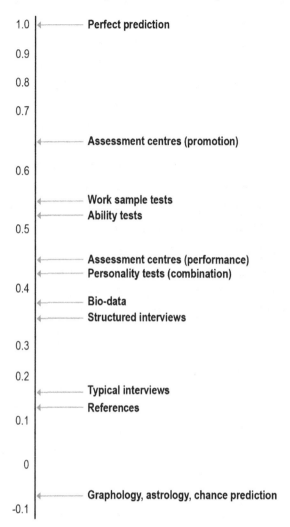

Source: Michael Armstrong, A Handbook of Human Resource Management Practice, 10th Edition, Kogan Page, 2006.

This chart taken from Michael Armstrong's handbook based on Stephen Taylor's work shows the predictive power of separate selection methods, i.e. how effectively we can assess a person's qualities that would be demonstrated once the person is employed. This overview also indicates the advantage of the assessment center (as a combination of several methods) and of the ability tests, and at the same time the poor effectiveness of prediction based on interviews, especially unstructured ones, and mainly on typical interviews.

Involvement of the Organization's Employees in the Selection Process

An example of involvement of the organization's people in the selection process is a case study from a Brazilian steel production company. The last step in the selection of the final circle of selected candidates is a semi-formal "selection lunch" with people from the micro-organizational unit in which the respective person would be working. During this lunch, the person is not asked any questions about his or her expertise; rather, the organization's people get to know the person through his or her personality, beliefs, and values. After the lunch, all participants from the organization answer just one question: "Would you work with this person?" To hire this person, regardless of all his or her other qualities, at least 75 percent of the replies should be positive. Such a method ensures observance of the existing organizational culture as well as the selection of people who support a similar value system to the one existing in the organization.

Source: Author's conversation with the owner of the company.

The STAR technique example in conducting a selection interview

This is a simple but powerful technique of conducting a selection interview that allows you to focus on and question in detail the targeted competency and behavior related to it. It can be used not only to assess the competencies necessary for the fulfilment of the requirements for the respective position (knowledge, skills, experience), but also the competencies necessary to fit into the existing organizational culture (beliefs, values, behavior). The technique consists of your guiding the person through four specific steps:

S—Situation

T—Task

A—Action

R—Result

This technique can be applied effectively only if complemented by the other two prerequisites for a good quality interview:

- Effective active listening
- Asking open follow-up questions, reflective of the active listening.

Example: Interview with a candidate applying to the financial planning and analysis organizational unit; the assessed competency is one of the organizational values—team orientation and teamwork.

/ *** /

S—Situation

Interviewer: One of our organization's key values is team orientation. Could you describe for me a situation which shows you are a team player?

Candidate: Yes, that was recently in my previous company when we were to prepare a work process development plan.

Interviewer (Follow-up): What kind of work process?

Candidate: Goods storage management.

T—Task

Interviewer: What was your role in this activity?

Candidate: My task was to analyze some of the financial indicators, to deliver them to the team, and to present part of the final plan to the management.

Interviewer (*Follow-up*): How come you had to present a part of the plan that is not part of your expertise?

Candidate: Part of the presentation I was making was related to the financial parameters (which is my area of responsibility), and I had had more opportunities than the other team members to present various things to the management.

Interviewer: Who decided on your role in the process?

Candidate: The financial analysis part was defined in advance by the project manager, while the financial indicators presentation to the management was my own initiative and suggestion to the team, so as to simplify the part which was less familiar to them.

A—Action

Interviewer: What did you do during that project that could confirm you are a team-oriented person?

Candidate: Hmm, many things. I went around and talked with all team members to establish the necessary analysis details; I tried to adapt to their obligations and understand what they were trying to tell me.

Interviewer (*Follow-up*): How did you show your understanding? What did you do?

Candidate: I tried to ask as many questions as possible and to listen to them, rather than speaking myself and making a priori conclusions.

Interviewer: What else did you do?

Candidate: During our meetings I tried to let the rest of the team present their part first and deliver my own part either towards the end or at the very end of the meeting. Several times I had to smooth some tense situations between the team members.

Interviewer (*Follow-up*): Why did you have to ease tense situations?

Candidate: I do not like it when tension arises, and I do not think it's constructive, either.

Interviewer: Can you think of any other performance which would confirm your team orientation?

Candidate: Well, I think the very fact that I offered to present the finance-related part, about which the rest of the team didn't know much, also shows my support for the team.

Interviewer: From today's perspective, is there anything you did not do or would do differently that would have been better for your team?

Candidate: Well, yes, I would insist a bit more on some of the indicators from my field of expertise.

Interviewer (Follow-up): Why didn't you do it then?

Candidate: In a way, I'm a bit hesitant, as I do not want to create any tension—not all indicators were unambiguous and simple.

R—Result

Interviewer: What was the final result of that project?

Candidate: Very good—the management accepted our proposals and was satisfied with the result.

Interviewer: In what way were you happy with your contribution to the teamwork?

Candidate: Well, from what I was told by the rest of the team, it seems I was of great help; they particularly mentioned that it meant a lot to them that I took over part of the responsibility for the presentation.

/ *** /

Such an approach to using the STAR technique accompanied by lots of active listening and follow-up questions provides a much more detailed insight into the concrete performance of a candidate (especially in Step A), and helps to assess to what extent the person's performance conforms with the competencies sought by the respective organization.

In the above example, if the organization fosters a culture where a person would gladly listen to others and support, help and try to understand his or her colleagues, this person could be a good-quality candidate. However, if the organization needs someone who would "stir" the team a bit, encourage different ideas and beliefs, and re-examine the quality of the team's decision, perhaps this wouldn't be the most suitable candidate. Such an approach, along with the STAR technique, undoubtedly provides a greater amount of information and a better quality assessment than questions such as "How would you evaluate yourself as a team player?" or, even worse, "Are you a team player?"

Five

Developing Our People

Imagine how much money we would spend on their development, and then—they'd leave the company.

—A board member of a multinational company, addressing the head of human resources development during a presentation of the budget for the following year

And can you imagine what it would be like if we didn't invest anything in them and they all stayed.

—The brilliant reply of the head of human resources development

It is difficult to imagine an organization in which there is no record or even an overview (perhaps a spreadsheet) where one could clearly see a list of the company's vehicles, especially the management ones, including their registration numbers, dates of registration and insurance renewal, due dates for oil changes, seasonal tire changes and regular servicing; the expiry date of the lease period may be listed, along with mileage and many other data.

But how often can we find such conceptually similar overviews concerning an organization's people, particularly related to recognized career development needs, planned development activities, expected development changes, successes, and plans? If people are the real and not just the declared value of a company, then why is it relatively easier to find a detailed list of the managerial car fleet than of its human resources? Every organization, even one with only a single vehicle in its management car fleet, also has a defined budget for the car's maintenance and, naturally, the higher the number of vehicles, the bigger the budget for their maintenance (and the likelihood of an officially allocated budget for their maintenance). At the same time, such an officially allocated budget can be found in an organization much less often when it comes to people development.

Even when both types of budget are available, the one allocated for managerial car fleet maintenance is bigger than the one allocated for people development.

Unfortunately, real-life practice once again dissuades us from, or simply confirms, what organizations regard as real value and what we actually label a value only for propaganda and political purposes because it is what is expected.

People development is still a category not really recognized in a sufficiently large number of organizations as a business need, something closely related to business success—an investment and not an expense, as it is often recorded in business books.

Why is the purchase of cars often recorded in financial reports as a type of increased value, while people development is generally recorded as expenditure? Moreover, once again we do not regard accounting as a set of established rules, but as a common-sense approach to reality.

In many organizations, it is still possible to find those, even among the highest-ranking, who question the need for people development (or even clearly express their negative attitude towards it). It is even more obvious in cases where a high-ranking person or even the owner of a company has climbed to that rank as a self-made man or woman, to whom structured or formal education has never been the basis or key to the realization of their business success.

Perhaps some light can be shed on the need for people development, or rather the insufficient understanding of this need, using the following three indicators:

a) The cost of hiring a new external employee—the total direct and indirect cost of the selection process as well as involving the person in the actual work—amounts to three to six months' salary of the position in which the person is hired. The further up this position in the organization's hierarchy, the closer the cost is to six rather than to three. Every time you have to hire a new employee, particularly because you lack a person with the necessary skills, abilities, and capabilities, ask yourself why this is the case. This, of course, does not exclude the fact that sometimes you will need to hire people externally despite any very intensive and valuable development activities involving existing staff.

b) Remarkably often, practice shows that when hiring people, companies pay their new people 15 to 20 percent more in comparison to situations where existing people are promoted to the same position from within. Besides the fact that this unfortunately very widespread practice brings additional costs, it also has a very negative effect upon the organizational culture. This is because the organization conveys the message that new, practically unknown outsiders are more appreciated than the people who already work in and understand the organization from within and have invested a part of themselves in it. Of course, sometimes there simply aren't any possibilities for good-quality promotion within the organization, and so a person needs to be employed from outside. However, organizations only rarely ask themselves why they have not had anyone to promote internally and whether they have perhaps failed in terms of active, targeted people development.

c) Having noticed the well-known fact that newly hired employees need some time to reach the expected performance standard, several global FMCG companies ordered a study that would verify the fact. The study showed that generally a newly hired employee of good quality needs on average 14 months to reach the level of performance of a good-quality predecessor in the same position. Interestingly, according to the same study, this period decreases by half when a standard good-quality candidate from within the organization is promoted to the position of a standard good-quality predecessor. Although the study does not quantify how the standard result falls short in these 14 months, it is obvious this is a question of underperformance or failure to deliver planned results.

A simple business calculation will clearly summarize the cost and value of the three specified elements:

- New recruitment (three-six months' salary)
- Hiring a new external person rather than promoting a candidate from within the organization (15–20 percent higher salary)
- Necessary time for the new person to reach the standard of a generally good-quality predecessor (14 months of underperformance).

All of the above elements constitute an expense—and not just a financial one at that—while the development of people is one of the key elements that could and should significantly reduce or eliminate some of these costs. People development within the organization is a clear business necessity. People development is a process during which we enable an employee to learn, practice, and apply new and different behavior.

Development has occurred only when change in behavior has also occurred and, in order to change behavior, it is necessary to focus on the cognitive part (knowledge, data, learning) and on the conative elements (beliefs, values, and emotions). Only successful work on all these elements can lead to behavioral change.

There are two major business reasons for people development in a business environment:

- It enables a person to perform the tasks and activities related to his or her current work position more successfully and efficiently.
- It prepares a person for how to perform the tasks and activities related to his or her potential future work position.

Development and its natural dynamics often collide with the required work dynamics.

Figure 10: Development and effect on performance

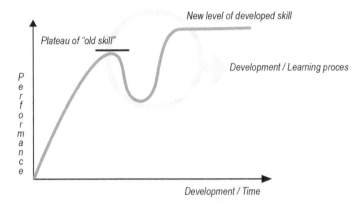

The development of each skill has its own natural course and, after we have developed it to a certain level, it is necessary to invest effort and energy in order to increase this level further. In the course of reaching this new level, the performance would be even weaker than the starting one because, to reach a new level, it is necessary to acquire some new elements and to improve on some existing ones. Usually, business does not tolerate this curve and is unwilling to understand it, since the firmly established approach in today's business world is that performance and efficiency should constantly improve.

Change of behavior, as a development determinant, seeks also the simple but demanding approach of the immediate manager. To make a person show they can behave differently, he or she should leave or should be detached from their comfort zone. The comfort zone represents all those situations that require a person to apply all they have applied up to that point and to behave the same way they have behaved hitherto. Taking a person out of their comfort zone puts them in a situation where they have to behave differently than they have until that moment, while persistent detachment from one's comfort zone develops and stabilizes new and different behavior, which leads the person into a new, higher comfort zone.

"Development" is often equated with the "promotion," and sometimes these words are used interchangeably as synonyms. However, they are two entirely different terms, processes, and even activities. The purpose of development is the improvement of business results of the job performed by an employee as well as possible preparation for a potential future position. Promotion is based on development and on a continuously good result shown in the preceding position. In spite of development, promotion may sometimes not take place (for example, if there is no room for promotion in an organization) but this does not necessarily mean there is no room for further development.

Environment and Development

Common sense, as well as experience, tells us that development is not equally successful in all types of professional environment. You are also familiar with the fact that in some companies, even micro-organizational units and environments, development occurs with exceptional ease and success, yet it is slow, unsuccessful or even completely absent in others.

An organizational climate answers the question of how people feel working in a specific organizational environment. It is possible to determine this using various and sometimes very complex and sophisticated tools and methods, but also in a relatively simple way: by asking the people within the organization for an answer to two simple questions:

1. The extent to which they feel (since organizational climate is an emotional category) the job they are doing is challenging and demanding.

2. At the same time, the extent to which they feel that they have or lack the necessary support (logistic, process-related, material, financial, human) for the job they are doing.

By combining the answers, one gets an overview of the various types of organizational climates, as listed in the following representation.

Figure 11: Developmental climate

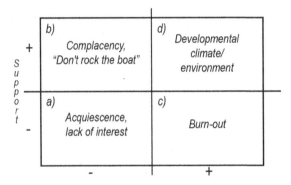

How challenging/demanding the job is

Results for the variable of challenge level will depend on the intensity of professional activities a person must undertake, the amount of energy they must invest daily, the complexity of work processes and how demanding the goals are.

Results for the variable of support depend on two basic elements:

1. Organization, type, and form of business processes, system definition, approved budgets, logistics, and financial support for completing assignments.

2. The immediate superior and his or her quality of communication, especially listening skills, understanding the position and the potential problems of people within the organization, active participation in development, team development, and understanding others, as well as personal issues.

Field a) describes a professional environment or climate in which assignments are most likely to be scattered, business goals are unknown or unambitious, and people's levels of engagement are low, with people at the same time feeling that, even for the small workload that needs to be completed, they are not supported enough by either the organization or by their immediate superior.

Such an environment is characterized by feelings of apathy, lack of interest, and resignation—an attitude that is then also applied to development and possible developmental activities. The need for development is not understood, questioned or recognized.

Field b) represents an environment and climate that anyone would, at first glance, desire. On the one hand, professional activities are not demanding, goals are attainable, and effort needed for completing assignments is not high, while on the other hand there exists all or most of the necessary support for performing such a job.

Although at first glance very enticing, in a developmental sense this environment is very demotivating. In the described environment, one can say that the "don't rock the boat" rule applies; why develop and aspire to better things when things are alright as they are? Development would only bring new and more demanding assignments.

Field c) describes a professional environment in which business activities are very demanding, invested effort needed for their successful completion is great, and business goals are high and very demanding, requiring strong everyday engagement. At the same time, the process of undertaking activities is missing one or more element of support—for example, undefined business processes, lack of necessary means, unclear responsibilities, lack of understanding, and lack of listening and support from the immediate superior—all of which requires additional investment of effort and expenditure of energy.

This type of environment and climate, although unfortunately very common, leads to the greatest depletion of people and, among all other types of climate, most often leads to burn-out. In such an environment, the primary focus is not and cannot be directed at development but rather at daily survival.

Field d) represents an environment and climate in which business activity is intensive, goals are demanding and challenging, and invested effort is significant, but this is an environment in which there exists all, or most of, the necessary support to undertake such assignments, as well as support given by the individual acting as the direct manager. Such an environment is the most fertile for people development and one in which the quickest and highest-quality development occurs.

Although profitable organizations cannot choose sides when the matter at hand is the job's demand level, this is almost always by definition a high level of demand and challenge: what the organization and the direct manager can and must influence is whether and to what extent they will position themselves in field c) or field d).

In order for the environment and organizational climate to be as motivating as possible for people's development, and in order for them to actualize themselves as much as possible through the features of field d), it is necessary to:

- Clearly define processes and business systems
- Define roles and clear responsibilities
- Secure logistic support for undertaking business activities
- Secure appropriate work conditions
- Secure necessary tools for undertaking business activities
- Secure budgets and financial support.

At the same time, it is equally essential (if not more so) for the immediate superior also to contribute to, and understand the importance of, supporting people's development and the creation of a motivational climate and environment by:

- Listening and developing honest, open communication
- Understanding the state of people within the organization
- Applying an appropriate leadership style both to individuals and to the team
- Providing quality feedback
- Providing personal support to members of his or her team.

The aforementioned determines that responsibility for people's development is first and foremost a managerial responsibility; it would perhaps be more accurate to say that each person's development is a joint responsibility of that person and his or her superior.

Competence as a Basis for Development

As already described in the chapter on selecting staff, competencies are also the starting point and basis for people development. In order to successfully and specifically develop an individual, we must determine certain criteria—competencies—whose development is essential if we want results and efficiency in the existing position or for the individual to prepare for successful entry into a new, future position.

Individual development must be focused and support the development and strength of key organizational capabilities; therefore, when determining individual competencies we must make sure they're in harmony with and stem from key organizational capabilities, or rather that the development of individual competencies supports the development of key organizational capabilities.

When defining competencies that represent the basis for development, it is essential, just as when recruiting, to understand that there are competencies that are easier and those that are much harder—in some cases even impossible—to develop. It is necessary to deal with the latter through correct and effective choices, while that should be primarily focused on those competencies which it is, at least partially, possible to advance and develop. Since the definition of development states that development has occurred only if a change in behavior has occurred, it is essential to define and describe, within the definition of competency, desired or targeted behaviors, which also describe competency in its visible and perceptual form.

Behaviors that describe competency enable an assessment of competency development based on visible and tangible examples and changes, but also describe which expected behaviors these are, or rather what a competency should look like when development occurs.

It is usual, especially when development is in question, to divide competency as follows:

1. Technical, operational, or functional competencies— often also referred to as *hard* competencies
2. Social, psychological, or human competencies that need to be developed to a certain degree in each individual within a social environment such as company or organization. These are often also referred to as *soft* competencies.

Both types of competencies are essential for every type of work position, and are, along with leadership and managerial competencies, assessed for all leading positions.

Technical or functional competencies are the level of education, knowledge, skills and experience essential to successfully perform certain clearly defined demands and position requirements or, rather, they secure expertise in professional action.

Some examples of *hard* competencies are:

Marketing
- Advertising techniques
- Knowing the market
- Drawing up a marketing budget

Finances
- Knowing accounting regulations
- Knowing and using the ABC method in accounting
- Drawing up an investment plan

HR

- Knowing and using selection tools
- Understanding and helping to manage organizational culture
- Using and developing techniques and tools essential for talent development
- Drawing up budgets for professional training

Delivery driver

- Possessing a "driver's license" for a certain category
- Knowing basic mechanical procedures
- Experience in contact with the end user.

Soft competencies are knowledge, skills, attitudes and emotions essential for successfully functioning in a socio-psychological environment, usually applied to every individual within the firm differently. Within this group of competencies one can find many that are difficult to develop, and these should consequently be secured through quality selection as the presence and development of these competencies has a significant influence on organizational culture.

Examples of some *soft* competencies often used within business environments are:

- Successfully functioning within a team
- Knowing and using communication skills
- Focus on the client (internal and external)
- Focus on the goal
- Caring about quality.

Managerial competencies are a possible third set of competencies and represent knowledge, skills, attitudes, emotions, and values that are essential to successfully undertaking managerial assignments, particularly those relating to control–leadership elements of management positions.

Typical managerial competencies in a business environment are:

- Strategic focus and understanding strategy
- Leading people and a team
- Conflict resolution
- Perseverance
- Providing feedback
- People development
- Resource management.

Specific developed and present managerial competencies have an exceptionally significant influence not only on the success of the company, but especially on its organizational culture.

When the matter in question is the group of managerial competencies that every individual in a managerial position should possess, it differs from competencies necessary for specialist and other non-managerial positions; it is common practice for competencies to be determined incrementally by their complexity and difficulty, depending on the hierarchal level of the manager.

This group of competencies is important not only for the development of individuals in managerial positions, but also for those preparing for a managerial position for the first time. A very common mistake within organizations is the promotion of people from specialist positions to managerial positions simply because they proved successful in their specialist positions. A common result of this is a situation in which an organization has lost an exceptional specialist and gained an unsuccessful manager or a manager of surprisingly poor quality. This happens because the promotion occurred based only on a set of competencies and results from the previous specialist position, while the need to prepare the individual for the new position was overlooked and the competencies essential for assuming the new managerial position were not developed. A top athlete is not necessarily a successful coach, just as many top coaches are not necessarily people who were top athletes. The set of competencies necessary for someone to be a successful athlete differ significantly from those that make a successful coach.

Determining Developmental Needs

Good and precisely defined competencies for each position are a strong foundation and a defined framework for employees' developmental paths, but they are, of course, insufficient for targeted and valid development.

Just as in other areas of business management, development must also be controlled, i.e. there has to be a reliable and valid way to measure the need for development. Without doubt, one of the most concrete indicators of a need for development is an individual's professional result. An unsatisfactory performance, one lasting for a period of time, certainly indicates a need for development unless a significant error in selection was made or the poor performance was caused by a significant decline in motivation. A result of insufficient quality is also a basis for recognizing areas in which progress/development is required, or rather room for improving an already good result. Besides business results, especially at an organizational level, developmental needs can also be recognized through frequent mistakes and oversights, analyses of business or workplace accidents, repeated failures, and so on.

A classic foundation and a conceptual basis for determining developmental needs is the competency set for an individual's work position. This approach "sharpens the image" of a specific area in which it is necessary to act for the purpose of development and better business results.

Therefore, in order to determine the developmental needs of people within an organization, it is necessary to compare and assess an individual for each of the competencies required for their position (technical/functional/soft/socio-psychological, and/or managerial, if the person is in such a position). The assessment is usually carried out using a numerical scale (1–5, 1–10, 1–100%) or a descriptive scale (where each level of development of each competency is described through behavioral examples). This author is a much stronger advocate of descriptive–behavioral scales as a change in behavior is not always best described in numerical terms.

It is important to view and value assessments of developmental needs, as well as the given grades, very differently from business results. The fact is that an individual graded with a low or lower grade for one competency is not necessarily a bad (or good) individual. Whether an individual within the organization is good or bad is indicated by that individual's professional result. A certain competency being assessed as poorly developed simply indicates a recognized developmental need and room for development in a certain area.

A very important and even essential element in people's development is the rule that development will not occur and people will not develop if they themselves do not feel or do not recognize that there exists specific room for development and advancement. It is impossible to command development. Consequently, it is crucial within the assessment of developmental needs to ask people to perform a self-assessment of developmental needs on the basis of required competencies. It is necessary to contrast and compare the self-assessment of developmental needs as a subjective but essential measure with assessments of that individual's developmental needs as recognized by people in his or her environment. For that purpose, it is necessary at least to take into account developmental needs assessments as prepared by the direct manager.

In order for actual development based on the assessments made to occur, the individual must comply with, become conscious of, and understand determined developmental needs. It is impossible to order the person to develop in a certain area, especially if he or she does not personally consider or understand why he or she should or must develop in that area. Consequently, each developmental need should be illustrated with examples of behavior from daily work, and arguments the individual may have for his or her self-assessment should be heard. Indeed, it is important to evaluate developmental needs from both sides (self-assessment and manager's assessment) and mutually synchronize recognized developmental areas. This process requires open two-way communication with mutual listening and acknowledgement, which allows the individual to recognize and determine developmental areas or even discover new ones, as well as allowing the manager to listen and understand the individual's perception of their own development and developmental needs.

The process cannot be set up in a way that imposes the developmental needs but, on the other hand, it is necessary to list the consequences that non-acceptance of development and neglect of developmental needs could have on one's result.

An expanded version of determining developmental needs at the level of employee-environment is the 360° assessment. 360° is a method in which developmental needs for a defined group of competencies are assessed by the individual, his or her superior, colleagues from the same organizational level, subordinates (if he or she has them), and even clients with whom the individual is in direct professional contact. Such an approach allows for comparison and confrontation of the individual and their subjective perception of themselves (self-assessment) with an "objectified" perception of developmental needs gathered from numerous people in the individual's environment. Results obtained with the 360° method have great power and strength to confront an individual with their own perception so that they confirm existing areas for development and/or become aware of unrecognized ones.

Besides precisely defined competencies and valid and reliable scales, which will be used in assessing the development of each competency, in order to use the 360° tool successfully, good preparation of all those involved is essential, as is the involvement of specialists who are very experienced and skilled in interpretation of the results obtained. It is almost an unwritten rule that results of the 360° method are better interpreted by people who are not members of the organization to which the method is being applied. Individual results can be compared with all others as a whole but can also be compared separately with every group that assessed the individual. The difference in assessment between different groups of assessors is certainly significant and serves as additional information about the possible developmental needs of the individual; for example, implying that the person acts differently with different groups of people or those at different hierarchal levels.

It must also be emphasized that the complexity of the 360° method makes it expensive, and it is thus not used extensively in practice. Most often it is used only for assessment of the developmental needs of the managerial sector, specialists in high positions, or significantly talented individuals.

In the business world—much more so than in, say, sports—there exists a tendency for a negativistic approach to development. In recognizing and determining developmental needs and later defining developmental activities, a much greater focus is directed at those areas in which an individual is weak, underdeveloped, or maybe lacks talent at all.

Much less energy and focus is directed at those areas in which the individual is strong and/or talented; those areas most often leave no room for discussion of the individual's development. Such a negativistic approach leads to the advancement and development of competencies in which the person is weaker and has weaker potential, while those areas in which the person is especially strong and/or talented are overlooked, not discussed, and underdeveloped. Such an approach to development in the business world produces mediocrity, not champions.

Business results would be much better if much more attention and energy were focused on the development of people's strong suits and not only on the elimination or reduction of their weak points. It is not weak points that help an individual to achieve something and succeed in life, but talents that make us successful in some area, activity, or line of work. Naturally, this is not to say that one should not work on eliminating weaker points.

Sport Inc.'s Story

Picture the company Sport Inc. and two people within it: Blanka Vlašić (high-jump athlete, multiple world champion, European champion, Olympic silver medalist) and Ivica Kostelić (skier, multiple Olympic silver medalist, world champion, winner of the World Cup). Both of these individuals work in their respective jobs, and their "business" result is measured through the achieved professional success. Since this is a company focused on sports, key competencies for all people within the organization are the same: team sports, swimming, gymnastics, athletics, running, high jump, tennis, long jump, skiing, and martial arts. If we were to apply the approach that companies use most often to develop people today, we would very probably discover that one of the most significant weaknesses or areas for development in Blanka Vlašić would be skiing and that one of the greatest weaknesses or areas for development in Ivica Kostelić would be the high jump. All energy for their development and creation of developmental activities, according to today's widely accepted approach, would be invested in Blanka Vlašić's skiing and Ivica Kostelić's high jump—and they would never become world champions in these disciplines but rather mediocre athletes.

Of course, weaknesses must be determined and corrected as much as possible, but it is much more important to determine strong fields and talents—those elements in which employees can give their maximum—and intensify their developmental activities in those areas; it is then that we will develop people in the most efficient way. A simplified rule could read: Determine weaknesses and try to correct them to an acceptable level; determine talents and focus most developmental activities on their further development. Then you will have the greatest success in developing people.

The way of determining developmental needs described thus far relates primarily to development and advancement of competencies necessary for successfully tackling the demands of an existing position. Besides that, development occurs in a way that prepares a person for a position to which they may be promoted in the future through developmental activities. Determining developmental needs for a future position requires a different approach to the one described thus far. When assessing developmental needs for a future position, the individual must be compared against the set of competencies for that future position.

If we assess the developmental needs of a specialist we are planning to promote to first-level management on the basis of the competency set needed for successful performance in his specialist position, we would be making a significant mistake for that person's development as well as in determining the developmental needs of that person.

For the sake of this specialist's successful development, it is essential to determine developmental needs on the basis of the competency set of the new managerial position. Since the individual has not worked in this new position, the method for assessing their developmental needs is different from those mentioned thus far. As there is no experience of the new position, not even in the competencies essential for successfully meeting its demands, developmental needs are determined at the level of verifying the potential. Of course, some already displayed behaviors and competencies are also relevant to the future, and are consequently easier to assess, but new ones the individual has never had a chance to use are assessed most often by the use of psychometric tools (tests, questionnaires), interviews (the STAR principle) or using the assessment center method.

The assessment center has already been described in the chapter on selection. The basic principle and purpose of this method is to place the individual in positions that mimic real situations and require the assessed individual to display competencies important for undertaking the assignments of their new position. The additional strength of the assessment center is that the individual is simultaneously observed and assessed by multiple expert observers, who in that way "objectify" the image of the individual's potential. The method also enables comparison of several candidates at the same time, and hence, in addition to providing a very detailed definition of developmental needs, it affords the opportunity for a more accurate selection of the individual ready for promotion.

The assessment center enables the precise establishment of behaviors and competency manifests that should and can be advanced and additionally developed. Because of its complexity and expense, this method is mostly used only for higher or middle management, or exceptionally important specialist positions. After each assessment center session it is essential, without exception, to give each of the assessed individuals expert and structured feedback to enable a better understanding of his or her own developmental needs.

The assessment center is undoubtedly one of the most powerful tools and methods for assessing employees' developmental needs and is almost indispensable for the accurate identification of the developmental needs of a new position.

One other very useful (but unfortunately very seldom used) method for determining developmental needs is for the top management of a company to discuss and mutually determine the developmental needs of middle or lower management (depending on the company's size) and of key people within the organization. This is naturally done on the basis of and through the framework of a defined and clear competency set as well as reliable and valid measuring scales for each competency.

By following up on and using previously defined tools through mutual discussion, managers exchange information and assess the developmental needs of each of the assessed persons, not only those they manage directly but also those at lower levels in the organization and from other organizational units with whom they are in professional contact on a relatively regular basis. As their internal clients, managers are able to assess the development of the assessed people from that perspective as well but also acquire an image that is possibly less subjective (i.e. more detached) than when a person is assessed by an immediate superior. Such an assessment can represent an "inventory" of key personnel in an organization. In best practice this is done at least once a year and sometimes even every six months.

Assessments provided by this method are very valuable as a supplement to people's developmental needs. In addition, they put managers in a position of more active involvement in the development of the people and team they lead and directly manage. When managers discuss key subordinates with other managers, only a few would allow themselves to be of lesser quality or less prepared than their colleagues, especially when given the chance to hear information about his or her people from other managers, as well as to give his or her assessment of the key people from other units in the organization.

There is no one uniform name for this practice, and it varies from company to company, but frequently used terms are "employee development forum," "people review meeting," and "talent inventory review."

Good definition of developmental needs is a key step for correctly and precisely determining the activities that will correct recognized weaknesses but also enable the recognized talents and strong suits of each person to be strengthened.

Developmental Techniques and Tools

In development, a valid rule is one that is in its nature and structure very demanding and conflicting for those applying it (the immediate superior or person responsible for someone's development). This rule asks that, as an immediate superior, you are tolerant and lenient while simultaneously firm and uncompromising. Firmness and resoluteness are essential in relation to an agreed plan of action and its implementation in accordance with the agreement; the individual in the developmental process must at least attempt implementation of agreed activities. Tolerance and leniency relate to the results the individual will achieve in the developmental process through implementation of agreed activities. The individual has a right to make mistakes and an imperfect result (otherwise they would not need development).

This is, for the immediate superior, a very demanding and difficult position to be in, especially keeping in mind that it is the *result* that matters most in daily business dynamics—and the attitude to that result is uncompromising—while actions that led to the result, especially if it is positive, are tolerated as not important.

When (or before) defining developmental activities, it is necessary to return to the definition of development and once again emphasize that the key assumption for development is a change in the behavior of the person being developed. Indeed, development has occurred only when it is possible to identify changes in the behavior of the person.

However, practice somewhat contradicts this definition of development. In almost all situations when you ask people "In what way did you learn or master most of what you know today and do at work?" the answer will be: with experience or through practice.

Still, it seems that few organizations use efficient practices to develop their people, while even fewer do so in a systematic and structured way. The most common alternative to a structured and systematic approach is trial and error.

There are countless ways in which competencies can be developed, depending on creativity, ingenuity and the capabilities of the organization and those in charge of it and of implementing development, i.e. HR and overall management.

Development ≠ Training

> Development is not (only) about training.

A very common understanding of development, and subsequently its usage within the organization, is one where development is synonymous with training; an equal sign is placed between the terms training and development. This is not even remotely true, and it is not justified to view the terms "training" and "development" as synonyms, especially as training is a relatively inefficient way of developing people.

If the previous sentence seems odd or even inaccurate, try to view things like this:

You have attended one or more training sessions at which the theme may or may not have been appropriate, the lecturer was or was not good, the material was or was not good, and the environment was or was not motivational; you returned at the end of the training to your daily job, put the materials in your locker and...kept doing what you had done until then.

Of course, this is not always the case, but it happens quite often. If we return once again to the definition of development as being a change in behavior, this happens very rarely (or not at all) during or after training. On the other hand, we cannot forget or neglect the basic purpose and benefit of training in a developmental sense, which is:

- Gaining basic knowledge in a certain area or competency
- Raising awareness of a particular area.

Nevertheless, training, especially if external and not adapted to the needs of the organization, represents the most expensive and inefficient method of people's development.

Training has its purpose, but it is not even remotely as powerful a method as it is considered to be, and real development begins or should begin only after training by applying and using what was learnt during it.

The knowledge afforded by training is welcome and essential for development to take place, but knowledge in itself is not enough for behavioral change, i.e. development. If knowledge were enough on its own, all smokers would stop smoking immediately because they know that smoking is harmful; however, although they know this, their behavior is not in accordance with their knowledge, and so they continue smoking.

Methods, tools, and developmental techniques are:

- Reading professional literature and or periodicals
- Congresses, seminars, conferences
- Workshops and training
- Formal higher education
- Market visits

- E-learning and M-learning
- Swapping positions
- Temporary employment
- Participating in a project
- Participating in expert panels
- Active project debriefing
- Mentoring
- Coaching.

There are more kinds of developmental tool and techniques than these and, as stated earlier, they depend on the creativity of those defining and implementing developmental activities, making the possible list of developmental activities practically infinite.

Developmental activities may be divided into:

A. Those that provide us with basic knowledge and/or awareness in a certain area.

B. Those that, through direct activity and inclusion, directly affect behavior and provide an experiential element.

A1) Reading various professional literature, books, periodicals, interdisciplinary journals.

This technique primarily affords the individual learning and acquainting themselves with new information a basic or supplementary understanding of certain job elements or awareness of a certain area of the job.

In essence, it is a cheap technique that does not require great financial outlay. Its efficacy is limited to adopting new data and supplementing understanding of certain elements, while it is more efficient if the reading material is recommended or provided by the immediate superior.

A2) Formal higher education (professional, undergraduate, postgraduate).

A tool or technique that initially enables the individual to get to know additional information and expand or deepen understanding in a structured and systematic way. This method only partly or in a very limited way puts the person in a position from which they must face real situations around them and/or gain actual experience. Because of this, it does not necessarily effect the change in behavior, although this too is possible. The aforementioned activities certainly cause changes in comprehension, and sometimes attitudes, which is a very important presumption for behavioral changes, i.e. development. Usually these are not cheap developmental activities—especially formal business education such as an MBA. Consequently, they are often used as a form of recognition and reward for those who have demonstrated exceptional results and are recognized as having significant potential for the company's future. Besides the cost, they also require a significant investment of time, as they usually last longer and consequently represent an additional demand for both the company and the people in it.

Environments that approach people development in a systematic and organized way do have development through additional formal education, but also have an obligation for those attending such activities to prepare and transfer ("cascade") the acquired knowledge to their colleagues through some form of workshop, lecture, or presentation, especially when the activities take place outside of the organization and are very expensive. In that way, the knowledge does not remain exclusive to one or a few individuals, but is spread to many people and becomes owned by the wider organization.

A3) Seminars, training, and workshops.

The most widespread, and often only, form of developmental activity in companies. Usually, these are focused on a narrow business sector or a specific competency and can range in nature from very passive to very interactive with intensive participation from the attendees. Their basic purpose is to provide basic knowledge and skills from a specific area, expand existing knowledge within an area, and/or build attendees' awareness of that area or competency. They may last from one to five days, allow numerous attendees to be present for the same topic at the same time, and are therefore a potentially cost-effective technique. However, this is not necessarily the cheapest method, especially if trainers are external, or if the content is generic and not covering attendees' specific developmental areas precisely enough. Moreover, we can consider it very expensive if nothing happens after training in terms of changes in attendees' behavior or the company approaching the matter systematically and actively, even though a shift in understanding and awareness is expected and, for the most part, does occur through such developmental activities.

By developing internal trainers—people recognized within the organization itself—and by precise definition of developmental needs covered by appropriate developmental tools, the efficiency of these methods and tools is increased.

Additionally, the efficiency of these tools can be increased, just as with previous tools, by the company insisting on a commitment to prepare and pass on a simplified program to colleagues after having attended training, workshops, and seminars, especially external ones. In this way, expenses are significantly lowered and those people who did not attend the developmental activity are enabled access to the information.

A4) Congresses, conferences, expert panels.

The basic purpose of these methods is to track new knowledge and information in a certain field, exchange experiences and refresh knowledge and thinking. Their main role is therefore additional awareness and only sometimes obtaining basic knowledge from a certain field. They enable an additional increase in understanding, and even alteration of existing personal experiences, as well as insights into both the good and bad of that which an individual/organization is currently doing. Usually they do not last long, and the financial engagement of the company is moderate in comparison with other techniques and tools.

A5) E-Learning (and M-Learning).

This is an increasingly present and widespread method, indispensable in today's society and very much tied to technological development. In its simpler forms, e-learning is little more than a digitalized version of paper educational equivalents, which enables simple forms of interaction (trial and error, receiving feedback on the correctness or incorrectness of acquired knowledge, comparison with other employees, etc.). In its more complex forms, e-learning enables multiple individuals to be involved in mutual (virtual) interaction and the development of knowledge and ideas through testing models and plans. Very sophisticated forms of e-learning enable, in an almost real way, not only acquisition of knowledge and experiences, but also the development of skills and enable adopted knowledge, acquired experiences and developed skills (i.e. realistic behaviors) to be tested.

The best examples of sophisticated e-learning systems are flight simulators, main bridges of large ships, and highly complex technological processes such as nuclear power plants.

E-learning, by its concept and design, is a developmental tool that belongs to the group of tools and techniques used to acquire new knowledge and raise awareness of a certain field, but also to the groups used to test and change acquired knowledge, develop skills, and gain experience, and therefore directly affects behavioral changes, i.e. development.

The cost-effectiveness of the e-learning method lies in its ability to be used when needed almost an infinite number of times. But every e-learning tool needs to be prepared, designed, and developed, which makes up the most expensive aspect of this tool's development, along with potential supplementary (also very expensive) usage tools. They consequently represent a potentially significant investment.

Today, e-learning is increasingly becoming m-learning (mobile learning), allowing the use of tools and techniques without regard to the physical location of the person in development, which certainly secures additional cost efficiency for this type of tool.

Another significant advantage of e-learning or m-learning as a developmental technique is its ability, very precisely and in a short period of time, to provide information on learning, the success of achieved results, and the type and frequency of errors made. This means that it can, most often and in real time, offer an extensive analysis of the developmental process and development itself. This developmental technique is extremely successful for the development of many competencies, especially in technical and professional areas, while it demonstrates its shortcomings in the development of psycho-social soft competencies.

As mentioned in the introduction to this chapter, the most common type of people development in a business environment occurs through experience or the conduct of real professional activities through action and work. Organizations do not utilize this fact enough by systematically using daily professional activities for the development of their people. When daily professional activities are used in a systematic and structured way targeted at people's development, they provide very strong development in real situations occurring in areas of real work.

Developmental methods and tools from this area are:

B1) Market visit/study visit.

A market visit is one technique that enables people to see, through visiting, how certain business areas and/or activities look in reality.

It is possible to visit different aspects of the same organization (especially if the company is a large one), such as various manufacturing facilities, markets, project meetings, and colleagues who are doing the same or a similar job, but also areas and activities within other organizations such as the markets and sales points of competitor companies, or a tour of business partners. The main purpose is to compare and expand one's own knowledge and experience and collect new ideas or alternative practices to later try to implement them into one's own work. This can last from one day to several weeks, and on rare occasions a few months. It is not necessarily a financially demanding technique, especially if carried out within the same organization. Its particular strength lies in the exchange of real experiences, tied to the same or similar experiences the person needs, and, if occurring within the same company and context and culture, a change in the observed and exchanged experiences is much more likely and easier. A presumption for quality here is to prepare the "host" of the market visit so that he or she presents and, as needed, additionally explains the observed experiences and practices as well as possible.

B2) Project participation.

Participating in a project, especially one that is new to the individual and in unfamiliar areas or in roles in which he or she has not previously participated, enables him or her, though such a professional and developmental activity, to receive basic information, develop necessary skills, acquire essential experiences, and advance those competencies recognized as a developmental need.

For these developmental activities to be successful, it is crucial that they be prepared and designed as developmental and not just professional activities. It must be made known which developmental need is intended to be developed through a certain developmental activity, what potential assistance can be offered (e.g. through mentorship), and in what way to measure not only the success of the project, but primarily the progress of the person for whom participation in the project served as a developmental technique.

B3) Peer development.

A very useful and in essence simple method in which colleagues in the same professional position or with very similar work transfer knowledge and experience to one another. This is a situation in which one person, most often very good at performing certain professional activities or competency, transfers his or her knowledge, skills, and experiences to another person for whom that competency has been recognized as a developmental need. In order for the method to be effective, it is essential for the person with the developed competency to prepare so that they know how to and are able to transfer the necessary knowledge and skills to the person from whom development in that same competency is expected.

After that, the person with the developmental needs should be allowed to spend some time at work with their colleague and observe and discuss real professional activities targeting the development of the recognized competency. Supported by additional education, discussion, conversation, and the possibility of asking questions, this method enables competency development right in the workplace. It is possible for two individuals with different competencies to find themselves in opposite positions. In that case, a "parallel" development of the two individuals with different competencies is possible in which one person transfers knowledge while the other acquires it, after which the roles are reversed.

B4) Position exchange (swapping).

A development method that is especially effective in cases of preparing an employee for a higher or more responsible position (advancing within the hierarchy) when they will be responsible for a wider area than they are currently assuming. This is especially appropriate when there are two or more employees within the organization recognized as potential candidates for promotion to a more senior position. This method enables the individual being promoted to collect necessary knowledge and experience from an area for which they were not previously responsible but will be after a possible promotion to a higher position. As well as enabling the person's development, it secures a simpler and more effective transition through the hierarchy. In the case of multiple candidates and their direct replacements, additional information about the candidates is received, e.g. an additional test for determining which person is more appropriate for the promotion to the more senior position.

In order for this method to be more effective, a somewhat broader preparation of those in the workplace is required, especially of the existing manager who will have to dedicate more attention to people who have switched positions. These new roles are less familiar to them, causing them to need support in their development through mentorship or coaching. If managerial positions are involved, such an exchange affords the people who have switched positions an opportunity, at some point, to lead people they have previously not led and to also get to know them better and have a better overview of the people they will, once they are promoted, be responsible for anyway. The question is often posed—if the position exchange involves two or more people recognized as candidates for a more senior position, what will happen to those who, following this activity, are not promoted? The answer is simple, and depends mostly on the organizational culture. In some organizations, the individual not promoted will experience disappointment and leave, while in others they will realize they have acquired expansion and opportunity, and will wait for another opportunity. Certainly, preparing a successor for those who have changed position amortizes and ensures a more successful transition, whatever the individual not promoted may decide.

Throughout the duration of the position exchange, it is essential that the existing manager has significant engagement with both candidates, whether in the form of mentoring, coaching, feedback, or short regular meetings with them. Simultaneously, i.e. in parallel, the organization will work at preparing a successor for these two individuals so as to successfully replace the one who is promoted, but also to prepare for the possible departure of the one who is not. This method, besides enabling development on the basis of direct activities and systems, secures at the moment of promotion a more efficient and simple transition, and will not be directed at only one familiar area (but rather removes the individual from their comfort zone).

B5) Assignment.

This developmental activity is in some ways a derivative of the previously described method, except that it is directed at one individual.

Assignment is a developmental activity that also has, as a primary goal, the expansion of existing knowledge and experience and/or preparation for a new or more complex position. In many organizations, there exists an unwritten or even formal rule that an individual who has been recognized as having potential cannot advance to, say, the position of senior director if they have not spent time in the sales or finance departments; or that they cannot be promoted to be marketing director if they have not spent some time in the sales department; or that, in order to be promoted to Training and Development Manager, they must have worked as an internal trainer.

Apart from the purpose of promotion, assignment serves to and is essential for expanding or refreshing knowledge necessary for one's current position. For example, every few months or years, a person in a senior position must spend a certain period of time in another professional function or sector.

Assignment can last anywhere from a few weeks to, at most, two to three years, and its purpose need not be exclusively developmental. In order to ensure the success of this activity, the organization must find a person to "cover" the position the individual in development has (temporarily) abandoned or reorganize professional processes and responsibilities, clearly determine developmental goals of the person on assignment, and assign a mentor, but also secure flexibility within the organization when the person on assignment returns to their "old" position, if that is one possible outcome.

B6) Action/project debriefing.

A method or tool for people development initially created not in a business environment but in a military (or more specifically, a war environment) although it is also used in sports.

The basic concept is that the team that worked on a joint activity or project must, at its conclusion, meet and discuss the result as well as what was learned from the activities conducted, whether these are positive or negative. These meetings and discussions, when well led and structured, are an opportunity to point out or confirm all that was done well and what can be used in the future, as well as behaviors and activities that need to be changed or done in a different way.

The basic idea is for the debriefing to take place while everything is still "hot," so that everyone is fully involved and interested (emotionally invested too) and therefore motivated for complete change or development.

It is recommended that the debriefing should focus not on negative elements, examples and behaviors—although these should not be left out—but rather on positive forms of behavior. It is possible that some positive behaviors occurred accidentally or not fully consciously. By pointing them out, we help people to become aware of any elements of which they were conscious and to use them again in similar or identical situations.

It is usual for the debriefing to be led by a superior but, for greatest success, active engagement by all participants is essential.

The debriefing should end with a concrete plan of activities which can and must later be tracked, measured and controlled.

Special Forms of Development—Mentoring and Coaching

Participating, in any way, in the development of his or her people is also development for the manager himself or herself, because transferring knowledge to others also means developing oneself.

Two forms or tools that have been mentioned several times in the discussion and descriptions of developmental tools thus far are mentoring and coaching. Both these tools call for the active (although different) engagement of the direct manager.

Mentoring

Mentor—Friend of Odysseus and Teacher of Odysseus's Son

This is a very common form of people development, especially during introductory periods and the arrival of an individual into a new company/environment or the developmental period after assuming a new position. The essence is that the person in development, or the one upon whom the mentoring is being practiced, has by their side an individual who is in some way responsible for their development during a certain period—a mentor. The basic principle of mentoring is that the person in development receives basic information and insight about their future position, and is acquainted with the basic demands of the position and the specificities of the professional environment, work assignments and activities, the organization, processes and procedures. The basic purpose of mentoring is to prepare the individual to undertake the tasks of the position they have just been given as well as possible. The goal of mentoring is to prepare the person for the range of the demands, without necessarily delving into the depth of development.

The mentor, as the responsible party, does not have to transfer his knowledge and information to the mentee directly, but must secure those people and activities that ensure the individual's necessary development. Naturally, the mentor and mentee must meet regularly and discuss their progress and development as well as further developmental steps to be taken, and the conversation must take a form that allows the person in development to pose questions and seek elaborations. The mentor must be a person whose organizational influence is such to allow all arranged developmental activities to take place in all necessary parts of the company. The mentor must also be prepared and educated about mentoring and his or her role in the process. At the end of the mentoring period, it is usual to assess to what extent the mentored individual has developed and actualized themselves through defined developmental goals. It is also very useful, at the end of the process, to assess the quality of the person who acted as mentor.

Coaching

In people development (or generally in management and dealing with people) if any definition has been mentioned, discussed, used, and wrongly used in the last few years (perhaps even decades), it is coaching.

Coaching is understood rather broadly, but it is unfortunately often misunderstood and interpreted as an activity carried out by external experts who possess the exclusive rights and skills for it, and as being exclusively reserved for top management and supreme talents. These external experts are most often called life coaches or executive coaches, or have some other attractive and somewhat mysterious title.

This approach may lead to several misleading assumptions:

- Coaches are educated specifically and exclusively, and the company's employees cannot coach.
- Being an expensive activity, not all employees can be coached, and such a developmental activity is exclusive to a select few.
- Coaching is performed in the form of counseling, giving and explaining (this is perhaps one of the most significant misconceptions of coaching).

Coaching is, in the opinion of the author, the most powerful developmental tool that can be present in an organization, but only if two basic prerequisites are met:

- The coach is a direct, immediate superior
- The coach knows and possesses the skill of coaching.

Coaching is primarily a process in which, in terms of development, a person is given a proactive position—which is why coaching is not guidance, counseling, proposing or any other form of "giving." Coaching is primarily about extracting, pulling out, and helping the person to find a solution alone instead of the solution being *offered* to the person; it is about making the person find ways or paths to solutions and activities. Because of this, coaching focuses on the coachee, the person receiving coaching, not on the person performing the coaching, i.e. the coach. It is about a person's development, and it is the person who has to take psychological responsibility and control over their development. Therefore, coaching is about extracting from a person, not about giving to the person, and consequently the responsibility is shifted to that person. (By contrast, when solutions are *offered*, responsibility remains with the person who is "giving.") The psychological sense of ownership over what the person has achieved on their own is different from the feeling when something is received from others.

Hence the possible definition of coaching: a developmental process in which the coachee is placed in a proactive position to reach the answers alone, a process conducted to help the person fully realize their capabilities and potential. Coaching is, accordingly, a process in which he who is hungry is taught how to catch fish, rather than being given a fish each time he gets hungry.

This is why coaching is different from "lower" forms of developmental activity, such as transfer of knowledge, or giving instructions, guidance, and counseling, because these are the types of development that put the other side into a passive position. Of course, this does not mean that these methods of development are not useful and welcome, especially in situations where a person adopts a basic fundamental knowledge of some area. But after a person has understood the basics, and is still not fully independent nor sovereign in governing a certain skill and knowledge, coaching is a tool that solves the problem very successfully.

When to Use Coaching

Coaching, being a very powerful or even the most powerful developmental tool, is useful in situations that most often represent a roadblock in the development of people within a business environment. If people development is analyzed, you will find that, in almost every organization, the most frequent roadblock or halt in development occurs when it is recognized that a person knows the basics and key elements have been mastered, but what is missing is a step towards independence, i.e. the successful independent performance of tasks, which is why the person still relies on answers, instructions and guidelines from a manager or a more experienced colleague.

The missing step to independence may be a lack of desire (i.e. motivation), but the cause may also lie in insufficient or incomplete understanding (i.e. abilities). And that is the crucial moment to use coaching. In some ways, coaching is a very powerful tool to "shift" a person from a position of knowledge to a position of understanding; or a tool for raising self-confidence and motivation.

Motivation and understanding cannot be ordered or provided, but you can help the person and "extract" from them one of those two key elements. Hence, coaching is used when you recognize that a person has the fundamental basic skills and knowledge, and that there is an initial motive, but one or both of these elements have not been fully developed.

Figure 12: When to use coaching

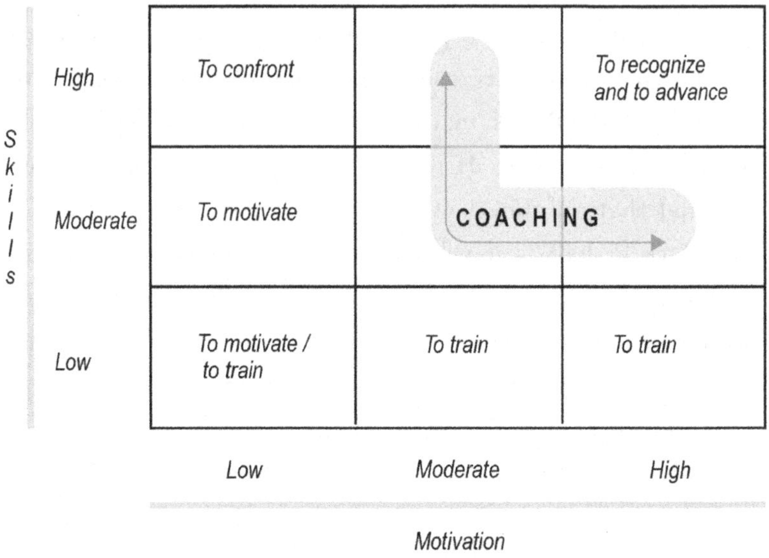

		Low	Moderate	High
S k i l l s	High	To confront		To recognize and to advance
	Moderate	To motivate	COACHING	
	Low	To motivate / to train	To train	To train

Motivation

A very common mistake, and even a reason for managers' confusion when it comes to the development of their people, stems from the comment that you may hear within an organization: *"I told them a hundred times how to do something, and they look for an answer for the hundred and first time."* Although seemingly justified at first glance, the comment also shows who is responsible for such situations. If you answered a question a hundred times, so you have trained that person to seek answers from you a hundred and one times. Many who have experience in leading people will react to that in the following way: "Yes, I'm aware that this is how things happen, but unfortunately I have no time to do it differently." This is in no way true, because if you had the time to repeat the same thing a hundred times, you seem to have all the time in the world at your disposal.

Coaching is, of course, a process that initially requires more time, but when good coaching allows a person to understand or find a motive, i.e. to become independent, you have saved yourself time in the future, at least when it comes to a particular task or skill.

How to Conduct Coaching

The first prerequisite of good coaching is a different way of communication, one that will place the person in a more active position. With advice, guidance, and counseling, the communication is more one-directional, and places a person in a passive position. Coaching as a process of development requires communication that will place the person in a more active position, for which two requirements are necessary:

- Active listening
- Maximum and qualitative posing of open and in-depth questions

The 80:20 golden rule of communication applies to the process of coaching: the coach spends 80 percent of the time actively listening, and 20 percent of the time asking questions. This ratio also applies to some business talks when you want to learn as much information as possible from the other side, i.e. put them into a more active position, such as in a selection interview or sales call. To achieve this ratio (70:30 would not be a problem, but in no circumstances can it be 50:50), the coach must understand the person's current position through active listening, and help him or her to reach a solution independently with questions. The crucial communication tool of good coaches is the questions raised, and active listening is necessary to make those questions sufficient and good. Active listening is particularly important or a crucial prerequisite for good follow-up questions, as they make the other side "sweat," or think differently and try to find a solution.

Coaching as a Cycle/Process/Method

Although coaching can be a one-off activity, in principle it is a process that requires several meetings, and it can hardly help if only one meeting is held. Coaching is a process, and above all a process whose basic elements correspond with a process of change management. By coaching, you must take a person through certain steps of the process, help him or her identify the target/destination they want to reach, help him or her analyze the current situation and understand its shape (and through a perspective they have not previously thought of), and then on the basis of these elements to determine what action to undertake so as to get from the current situation to the desired goal.

One of the key elements differentiating coaching from a friendly conversation over a coffee is that each coaching meeting must end up with a clearly defined and firm plan of activities.

And while the process of coaching is such that the person is placed in a position of better understanding, awareness, greater motivation, or better structuring, the development defined as a change in behavior will occur only after the coaching—by applying and implementing the established action plan, now easier and more successful because of the increased understanding and/or motivation.

For the purpose of control, when coaching is set up as a regular process and system, each subsequent coaching meeting should begin by revising the plan of activities agreed at the previous meeting. Following the revision, it will be possible to determine either that the developmental need and area are sufficiently developed and that a step forward can be made into a new area, or that further and deeper work on the existing developmental need is required.

The methods used in coaching are numerous and diverse, and one of the simpler, more effective, and thus probably widespread is GROW. This is nothing more than an abbreviation of a four-step process through which you guide and "drag" the person being coached.

G (GOAL) – Setting up and defining the developmental goal

R (REALITY) –Analysis of the current and past conditions that brought about the developmental need, and analysis from a different perspective

O (OPTIONS) – Generating, evaluating and selecting options that it is believed can help the realization of the developmental goal

W (WILL, WORK) – Definition of a clear final action plan, which it is believed will help the achievement of the developmental goal, but also identification of the motivation of the person coached for carrying out the activities agreed

Like the STAR principle in the selection interview, the GROW process must be supported and accompanied by an abundance of listening, high-quality open questions (follow-up) that help the person reach solutions without your counseling, directing or giving answers.

Table 5: Comparison between coaching and mentoring

Mentoring	Coaching
More informal meetings whenever required or when opportunity arises	Structured and regular meetings
Looks at the person from a broader perspective, extensive development	Focused on specific developmental areas, in-depth development
Mentor usually transfers their experience and is senior to the person	Coach may have no specific knowledge, but must know the specific process of coaching
Focused on career development	Focused on specific business needs
Preparation for the performance of future roles	Preparation for the performance of current specific objectives and tasks
Refers more to the expertise of the mentored person	Refers more to specific developmental problems
Primarily the process of giving, referral and counselling	Primarily the process of "extracting" from a person

Feedback

Every process of development becomes more difficult—sometimes blocked—if not accompanied and supported by positive feedback.

The quality of feedback aimed at developing people largely contributes to the development of each person. Although feedback might have many different justifications and purposes, the key principles of giving feedback for developmental purposes are:

- Before you give feedback, ask the person what he or she has to say and think about what you intend to give feedback on. Once the person expresses his or her opinion about what you should provide feedback on, the person will listen with more interest and motivation to what you have to say. If you start giving feedback prior to asking what he or she thinks, the person may view your feedback as a monologue and, as a result, it will not be listened to well enough.

- Feedback must be provided as soon as possible after the situation or activity to which it relates. If the feedback comes very late, it can have two negative effects:
  - o The person forgets what the feedback refers to, while you also cannot clearly remember all the details required for good feedback.
  - o The person is additionally frustrated, particularly by late *positive* feedback, because they note how long you took to provide it (especially if you always provide negative feedback immediately).

- Feedback must be conveyed as an explanation of specific behavior—supported with facts, results and actions—and not through general and common statements, even if they are positive. "You're smart" sounds good but says nothing about what a person has done well to be considered smart. "The way in which you analyze results and lay out the report is really meaningful and very useful" would be much better developmental feedback.

- When feedback is positive (which is especially important for the person, but also for the group of people with whom they work), it is desirable to provide feedback in the presence of the others—as an example for them and as a motivational element for the person. However, do not overdo it, because the inflation of such feedback in front of others leads to the loss of importance and effect of such feedback.

- Never give negative developmental feedback in the presence of others if your key intention is the person's development. When you start giving feedback to a person in the presence of others, after the first negative word the person will not actively listen, either to you or to the remaining feedback, but rather think about the social situation and the discomfort you have created by providing feedback in the presence of others, and about what others now think of him or her.

- When providing developmental feedback, avoid discussing motivation, especially when the feedback being given is negative. The majority of people undergoing the development process do not *intend* to generate a bad result, so you will not receive any valuable information by analyzing motivation.

- When providing particularly negative feedback, make no comparisons between the person receiving the feedback and another person. People are generally aware if they failed at something, and that others were better; comparison with another person will only cause antagonism between the two.

- Particularly in the case of negative feedback, avoid the words "always" and "never." Even those who are often late are not always late and will sometimes arrive on time, while the statement "You are always late" causes a justified negative reaction and defensiveness because they will think of the occasions when they were not late.

- When presenting negative feedback, always avoid the so-called Friday afternoon effect. Do not wait for the right moment, which is usually delayed until the end of the week, thus making you give feedback on Friday so that the person can "cleanse" himself or herself over the weekend. If there are reasons for negative feedback, they are not likely to be resolved by themselves, and the more you delay providing such feedback, and negativities are not corrected, the more your emotional involvement and frustration will grow. When you give feedback in such a state, it will be everything but what it should be: without argument, explanation, or facts, but with plenty of emotion, frustration, and distorted judgment.

Developmental feedback is the essence of the development process and, along with sticking to the above rules, it must be provided through discussion with lots of questions and much listening and interactive communication instead of one-way speeches and monologues.

A very common form of feedback, known as the sandwich method, is extensively used in the Anglo-Saxon culture, although it is inappropriate for some other cultures. This is because when you begin to give feedback in many environments and cultures according to the sandwich method, in addition to the positive elements, the other side will be focused on your "however" and will be waiting for the negative thing you have to say. Until then, the person will not have the same level of active listening. On the other hand, addressing the positive and the negative together can be seen in many cultures as a kind of manipulation, leading those receiving the feedback to distrust it and not listen with sufficient engagement.

Talents: Recognition and Development

Every sports team is as strong as its bench, and this could also apply to the teams in an organization. One of the greatest qualities of successful managers is the identification and development of people who could be their eventual successors, or those who have the qualities to be promoted to more responsible positions. Very often, perhaps a bit pretentiously, individuals identified in this way are called talents. Although it is difficult to find a more appropriate and less pretentious name for these people, we need to be aware of the possible danger in deeming some people as talented, which could then be translated as deeming others talentless. Despite these risks and constraints, in further discussion we will use the term "talents."

The absence of a successor, particularly one properly prepared to succeed someone in a vacant position, causes various problems and significant costs—already been described at the beginning of the chapter on development (costs of hiring a new person, higher costs for newcomers, the time required for a newcomer to reach the predecessor's standard of work). The lack of systematic development and management of talents very often results in the best people leaving the company because they see no future for their careers and do not feel that they are developing and advancing in their jobs. This significantly hurts the organizational culture and reduces the EVP strength.

To recognize talents (individuals who are potential candidates for further development and advancement), these people must be monitored and evaluated through two variables:

- Results in their current position
- Assessment of the potential to meet the requirements of the future possible position.

An extensively used method in defining talents is the so-called nine-box grid tool, which assesses people through those two variables. Recognized talents are usually those who are positioned, after assessment, into one of the three fields in the top right of the matrix (shown below). It is important to emphasize that the central field of the matrix must not be underestimated or ignored, as in reality it contains the major proportion of important people.

Figure 12: Nine grid/box model

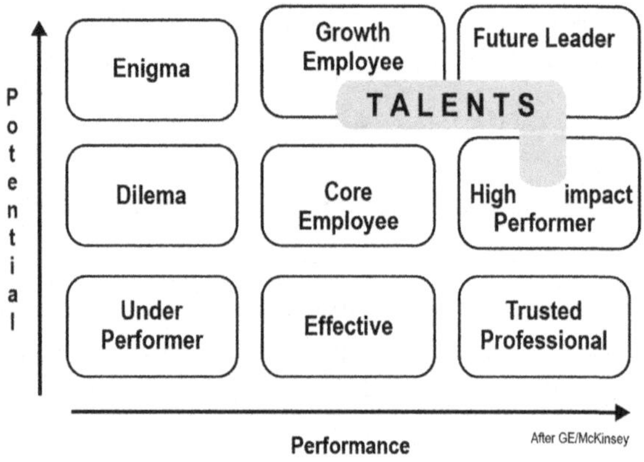

After GE/McKinsey

One of two axes is stronger and more tangible—the performance in the current position, which can be relatively easily and reliably determined. The other variable is the potential for success in performing the requirements of the possible future position. To determine this variable best and most accurately, the person needs to be assessed and compared against a set of competencies and requirements of the new position, projected into the future.

Successors and talents are people to whom you must clearly communicate that they have been identified as such—not in the form of promises but rather as an additional opportunity and form of recognition of their quality, and as acknowledgement of the additional energy, effort, and resources that will be invested in their development. In addition to the development of competencies that will enable the person to cope more successfully with the demands of a possible new job in the future, the successor also needs to be specially developed and prepared to fit into the desired organizational culture or as a leader of change in the organizational culture. For this reason, special attention needs to be paid to the values, attitudes and emotions of successors and talents, not just to their technical competencies.

People identified as talents are being developed not only to achieve better results in their existing position but also to be more successful when they assume the projected new position. Their development plan therefore also encompasses the improvement of those developmental needs assessed as existing and referring to the possible future position.

To be recognized as a talent does not mean having that status permanently and exclusively: in organizations that are good at this, this kind of recognition is performed on an annual basis, and in that period a person previously identified as talented may have peaked—in which case it would be better to keep them in the same position; or the person may have failed to deliver the results expected in the period or has only recently been promoted, in which case it is too early to reassess that person.

The immediate superior must be particularly actively involved in the development of successors and talents through all the aforementioned activities: the assessment of the developmental needs of these people, and training, counseling, mentoring, coaching, delegation, and regular and useful feedback.

Techniques of Assessing the Success of Development—Measures of Success

The success and effectiveness of developmental activities has to be monitored and measured just like any other business activity and process in a real business environment. Unfortunately, companies do not pay enough attention to this, or sometimes even ignore it altogether, regardless of how much money and effort has been invested in development.

Returning to the basic definition or concept of development, it is clear that what needs to be measured is behavior, or more precisely change in behavior. By its nature, this is a category that is difficult to measure simply and accurately (or at least we have not learned to do so), which is why organizations either give up on it or do it insufficiently well—with honorable exceptions. But we have to be able to measure it, just as we do any other business activity, because only then can it be managed. A similar concept applies to marketing activities: it is not always possible to define clearly the outreach of marketing activities towards the end result, and to what extent they are a consequence of other business and out-of-business activities. However, marketing and marketing activities are regularly and continuously measured so as to be managed.

Baseline Measurement—The Starting Point

Before the implementation of important and comprehensive developmental activities, it is necessary to evaluate the existing state of development of competencies to which the future developmental activity refers—the baseline measurement.

Baseline measurement is by its structure similar to the definition of the developmental needs of individuals. This means that competencies are measured in their behavioral form, with the use of evaluation scales describing behavior in grades, rather than by using nominal scales. Besides measuring competencies, the baseline measurement can (and indeed should) measure some elements of organizational cooperation, team dynamics and organizational culture/climate, but also business results.

Baseline measurement will provide a more accurate and objective evaluation of whether developmental activities have caused a change in behavior and, if so, in what direction and to what extent.

Levels of Measuring Development

Development, i.e. the success of developmental activities, is mostly measured through four levels:

- Satisfaction with developmental activities
- Adopted/new knowledge
- Changes in individual behavior (actual development)
- Business results.

Measuring Satisfaction with Developmental Activities

This is the most often-used method in evaluating developmental activities. Unfortunately, it has the lowest value in measuring actual development, i.e. the change in behavior. In fact, it does not measure the change in behavior at all. It is used very often after training sessions and workshops, for example by asking participants to evaluate the program elements (e.g. the value of content, transfer of knowledge method, quality of lecturers, materials used and training materials, evaluation of applicability in practice, etc.).

The significance of this kind of evaluation is often overstated, and unfortunately in many areas it is used as the only evaluation of developmental activities.

This type of measurement primarily or almost exclusively measures the participants' satisfaction with the developmental program and the importance of information acquired through this method. However, this says nothing about the development of the participants themselves, the knowledge they have gained, or the behavior they have changed.

Measuring the Adopted or New Knowledge

This is very often a formal process, which puts participants in a certain developmental activity in a position to demonstrate new knowledge they have adopted. It is usual to conduct it immediately or sometime after the completion of the developmental activity, in the form of questionnaires or tests, or in the form of testing in an actual situation (or, in the case of e-learning, a virtual one). A derivative of this method is that participants who undertook certain developmental activities are given the task of preparing the same training or developmental activity for another person or group. This puts them in a position to learn the subject in more detail.

The method defines the knowledge that is or is not acquired and to what extent, both at an individual and a group level, and allows correction/redesign of the developmental activity in those areas that were insufficiently mastered. Despite the good information it provides about the knowledge gained, this method cannot provide precise information on the change in behavior, i.e. actual development.

Measuring Changes in Behavior—Actual Development

This is probably the most reliable and valuable method in measuring actual, real development. Usually this method measures behaviors in the same way as in the baseline measurement. Competencies are therefore measured and evaluated on the behavioral scale. After measuring, results are compared with the baseline measurement and the achieved balance is defined: the changed behavior, i.e. the development. And that is exactly where the value and quality of this method lie. It is also usual for such measurements not to be conducted immediately after each developmental activity but after a longer period, usually once a year, when developmental needs and advances in the development of competencies are defined on an individual level.

For this method to provide good, reliable results, training in evaluation must be provided for those participating, most often immediate superiors, HR specialists and other employees.

The summarizing and grouping of individual grades provides an overview of the success of developmental activities within the entire company.

Measuring Business Results as a Measure of Development

This is a very valuable, but far from simple, measure of the success of developmental activities: similar to the previously mentioned measurement of the success of marketing activities, there are many interfering factors that might impact the end results, which is why it is difficult to define precisely the direct impact of developmental activities on the business result. Some of the numerous interfering factors that can occur between the development and business results are: increased experience of the person during the monitored period; success, failure or change of the immediate superior (which can affect motivation); team dynamics; reorganization or new methods of work; and market changes.

Despite these potential limiting factors, developmental activities and the business result must be correlated because development does occur in a business environment achieving better business results.

Some measures of development and development activities are methodically very developed, although not very often used as ROI (return on investment) on development.

Such methods require practice and expertise, which is why it is best to leave them to the HR experts.

Organizations need tools, systems, and processes to get managers interested in active involvement in the development of talents. For example:

- The development plan must be an integral part of the overall business plan and thus directly affect the managers' interest in the analysis, preparation, definition and implementation of developmental activities.

- Development as one (or more) of the KPIs for each of the immediate superiors. Good business practice recognizes developmental activities as integral elements in the personal business goals of all managers. In particular, this relates to the development of talents and successors, one of the direct managers' KPIs which refer to recognition, identification of developmental activities of recognized persons. This KPI is treated like any other, but in some cases has a higher relative weight than the "usual" KPIs.

- If each KPI includes clearly defined Performance Management and a clear connection between the achievement of business goals and the reward system, then the total prize/bonus earned in this way also depends on achieving the goal related to the development of people and/or recognition of talents and successors.

- The immediate superior is actively involved, as a member of management, in group discussions (people development forum, talent review meeting, talent management meeting) and thus discusses not only the developmental needs of his or her people, but also all the company's the key personnel.

- Another way to interest immediate superiors in the development of their successors is to introduce the practice and rule that you cannot progress unless you have developed the person who is to succeed you. In this way, managers have a direct and personal interest in developing the person who will be successful in succeeding them.

- Formally established and defined systems of mentoring and coaching require immediate superiors to be directly involved in the development of their people, especially of identified successors.

An immediate superior and his or her involvement play a crucial role in the development of people within the organization. An immediate superior is the directly responsible person (an aspect that comprises part of the managerial role and responsibility), or is at least jointly responsible, for the development of his or her own people. An immediate superior must be supporter, facilitator, trainer and coach to his or her own people and have at least a 50 percent influence on the team's overall developmental climate, as mentioned at the beginning of this section. The role of immediate superiors is to help, but also to persist in the development of their people.

An immediate superior participates in the development of his or her own people as a manager by:

- Jointly creating developmental tools, processes and procedures that ensure the development of all people in the organization.

- Budgeting for providing the resources required for the development of people.

- Actively participating in the evaluation of the developmental needs of his or her people based on competence, and using the agreed tools (e.g. the 360° evaluation).

- Regularly carrying out agreed developmental activities (mentoring, coaching, training).

- Controlling the implementation of agreed developmental activities.

- Measuring the progress achieved through developmental activities and defining new activities required.

- Ensuring that the present structure of KPIs has a section relating to people development.

Immediate superiors as leaders participate in the development of their people in the following ways:

- Their behavior is a model of how important their own development is, but also the development of the people managed.

- Create a climate and environment in which development is of maximum quality.

- Identify and understand the talents and weaknesses of their people.

- With their people, openly discuss their talents for and limitations on development and provide arguments through concrete examples and behavior.

- Constantly require others' feedback on their developmental needs.

- Use every opportunity to provide others with good developmental feedback.

- Ensure that developmental activities are implemented, while at the same time being tolerant about the results achieved during development and developmental activities.

- Jointly with their people, set out the required developmental activities.

- They are true coaches to their people.

- They do not command the development of people, but clearly explain the consequences of non-development.

- Openly and actively recognize and continuously develop their successors, and are proud of them.

Examples, Tools, and Research

CIPD research

A 2011 study by CIPD (the Chartered Institute of Personnel and Development) of dozens of companies with a structured Talent Development Program demonstrated the importance of coaching, mentoring and structured feedback, as evaluated by 302 respondents representing the people most valuable to the organization's future—the talented.

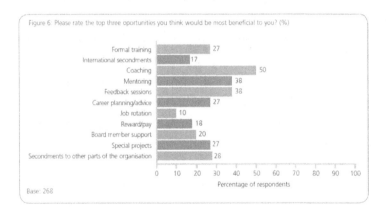

Figure 6: Please rate the top three oportunities you think would be most beneficial to you? (%)

Base: 268

Source: "The Talent Perspective: What Does It Feel Like To Be Talent-Managed?" CIPD, London, 2010.

Making coaching work

Here is a list of tips and advice to help you coach more effectively. They are not a panacea, but should help you avoid the most common mistakes.

- Don't over question—it's not an interrogation
- Summarize often
- Be aware of double pressure on you—your preference for giving advice and the coachee's request for advice

- Resist giving advice prematurely
- Try to offer reframes and different perspectives through questioning
- Remember that coaching should lead to action
- Identify restraints, especially internal ones
- Check whether the issue is a puzzle, problem or dilemma
- Balance your reality questions with questions which move the issue on
- Remember to use the naïve question
- Understand the emotions as well as the logic
- Challenge if necessary, but learn how to challenge elegantly
- Use "what if" questions
- Ask how important the issue is
- Build on what the coachee is actually saying, rather than inventing new questions
- Pick up on non-verbal communication. Notice if people get excited, or sad
- Use more open than closed questions.

Source: Mike Brent: "Coaching for development," The Ashridge Journal, www.ashridge.com/directions, Spring 2002.

Coaching as a System within an Organization

As stated earlier, coaching is a tool that generates its greatest and best results if the coach is the immediate superior and knows how coaching works.

This means that coaching provides the best results if regularly performed by all immediate superiors with their people, i.e. if coaching is introduced into the organization as a system. The successful introduction of coaching in an organization requires the following steps:

1. Introduction of coaching as a system within the organization must be a managerial decision made at the highest level, and only then can it be successfully implemented.

2. Accountability to conduct live coaching as a system must be accepted by all managers within the organization, and HR (if such a function exists), must assume operational responsibility for helping in the system's introduction.

3. All people, including those who are not future coaches but will be coached, must be informed about the introduction of the system.

4. All included in the system as future coaches (immediate superiors) must be trained and educated on how to conduct coaching.

5. Individuals—internal coaches, but not necessarily only those in HR positions—who will be present at the initial implementation of the system at coaching sessions, undergo additional training, monitor the performance of coaching meetings and, after completing the coaching meeting, help coaches by providing feedback on how well they coached.

6. The effective introduction of any system, including coaching, in an organization requires determination and discipline. Consequently, and in accordance with good practice, the dynamics of coaching meetings must be defined at senior levels within the organization, as well as the schedule of coaching meetings over a long period of time:

   a. The dynamics of coaching meetings increases in line with the operational dynamics of the business, so that at the organization's lower levels coaching meetings are to be held more often, and at the highest levels significantly less often. Good practice suggests that the highest level managers hold coaching meetings with each of their people every quarter (or, usually, every two months), while middle management has a frequency of one coaching meeting with each of their people every one to two months, and at the lowest organizational levels coaching meetings are held every 15 to 30 days.

b. Creating the schedule of coaching meetings for the entire organization (with the exact date and time) between six and 12 months in advance serves the purpose of discipline and planning, and can also provide social pressure to get the system established.

7. Each coaching meeting should leave a written trail for the action plan, and during the early stages it is good to send these records to the person with whom the coaching meeting was held and to an individual in an HR position, who can thus control the implementation of the system both qualitatively and quantitatively.

8. Internal coaches should attend coaching meetings during the system's implementation and customization to monitor the method and quality of the meetings, and after each meeting provide feedback to the coach about the quality of the meeting and any room for improvement.

9. As with any other system, implementation needs to be measured, and this is the role of those in HR positions. Measures include:

a. Quantitative, strike rate—the number of coaching meetings held in relation to the number of scheduled meetings within a period.

b. Qualitative—this can be drawn from the forms completed at the end of coaching meetings or by additional formal evaluation of the quality of coaching meetings by internal coaches when they attend coaching sessions. The best qualitative measure is to measure and compare the development of competencies (especially those specifically covered by the coaching process) the beginning and the end of the period, usually one year apart.

10. As already mentioned (but it bears repeating), implementation and living of this process should be classified as a management accountability, and the process will be implemented as long as the top management, especially the most senior person, is actively involved in the process, i.e. by holding good coaching meetings with their people on a regular basis.

Building a "pathway" to leadership

ANZ, a leading Australian bank and financial services provider, set out to transform itself into a "super-regional bank," focusing on achieving aggressive growth outside its home markets of Australia and New Zealand. To meet these goals, ANZ had to ensure that its leaders had the distinctive set of capabilities necessary for the transition.

The first phase of the program built the foundation for organizational leadership in the region through the development of a unique ANZ leadership model with the full commitment of senior executives. The model identified leaders at all levels and critical leadership transition points. The competencies necessary for success were aligned to the new super-regional strategy and leadership model, and the company designed a "leadership pathway program," including a set of bespoke learning programs for each leadership level, to support the development of super-regional leaders through enhanced leadership and business skills.

In the second phase, the pathway program was deepened through the adoption of an informal online learning tool implemented widely across the bank. A generalist bankers program brought the new strategy to one organizational level; an executive leader program was required for senior executives; and recommended learning was introduced for first-time managers. A speaker series brought the strategy to life for all staff.

Currently in the third phase, the program has adopted a model of leaders teaching leaders with a renewed focus on identifying and targeting high-potential leaders for the executive leader program. Thus far, over 5,400 people have completed programs in the pathway, logging close to 110,000 hours of learning. Business results for the bank have continued to improve throughout the strategy's implementation. The bank is increasing its rate of internal leader promotions as well. Thanks to a high level of commitment to the strategy throughout the company, measures of employee engagement have risen significantly, and senior executives are actively building and demonstrating the culture change necessary to achieve the strategy's goals.

Source: Global Human Capital Trends 2014: Engaging the 21st-century workforce, Deloitte University Press, 2014.

The example shows that the development of leadership and successors, and through them the development of a different culture, is a complex and time-consuming process that requires management's full commitment and that of everyone in the organization, as well as appropriate process measurement.

Six

To Manage People by Mind and to Lead them by Emotion

When the power of love overcomes the love of power, we will open our eyes,

When the power of love overcomes the love of power, we will walk the right path.

ST!LLNESS, Croatian reggae, rock, dub, hip-hop crossover band

When the power of love overcomes the love of power the world will know peace.

Jimi Hendrix, rock legend

To successfully lead and manage people in the most positive sense, they need to get from you a balance of the rational and the emotional; they must understand, but also feel. To achieve this, act from both the position of a manager and of a leader.

If you are an immediate superior, your people will need the manager in you, one who will use his or her activities to create around *Homo sapiens* an environment that he understands. As a good manager, you will:

- Plan

- Organize

- Measure

- Budget

- Design

- Control

- Communicate.

You must use all the tools, systems, processes and procedures relating to people, their motivation, the method of their selection, their development, and the way of creating and maintaining a desired environment.

The manager is, consequent upon the similarities and differences between management and leadership, primarily a rational category, and people need all that a manager can do to place us rational beings into the context of the organization, its activities and its work, and have us understand all that needs to be understood.

Management is also power, and above all the power of position; the power whose strength lies in the possibility of punishing or rewarding someone because of that position. This power matters in the organization. Management (without leadership) uses power founded on fear, whether a person's fear of punishment or of not being rewarded by the superior.

Management is absolutely necessary in every organization, but excessive management or management without leadership implies too much of the rational, which can lead to neuroticism—both in each person individually and in the organization. Human nature needs more than reason and the brain.

Unlike management, leadership is a predominantly emotional category, and perhaps therefore has not been fully explained. Emotions cannot be reduced to the rational, which is anyway unnecessary because it would render them void.

When you are a leader to your people, you provoke emotion in them—not necessarily always or exclusively of a positive kind, but certainly the kind of emotion that builds up your power in their eyes and does not require a formal position for you to express it.

Real power derives from you and from what you are, and power that provokes emotion cannot always be explained. You can provoke a strong positive emotion only if you act from truth and from the fountainhead of all emotions: the position of love.

- When you act as a leader from the position of love, you are successful in the job you are doing and build successful relationships with the people you work with.

- When you act as a leader from the position of love, you sincerely and without reserve recognize and let people know that they have done something good, and then you reward them without reservation; but you also have no reservation about pointing out what was wrong and even punish them if necessary.

- When you act as a leader from the position of love, you are creating an environment (culture) that provides the best results for the organization and the greatest engagement of your people. You recognize and encourage those people and behaviors that support such an environment, but also protect and defend it by neutralizing and removing undesirable behaviors and people.

- When you act as a leader from the position of love, you choose the best for your team without exception, even those who are better than you. You admit that some were not selected well, and attempt not to repeat such mistakes.

- When you act as a leader from the position of love, you are fully and without reservation dedicated to the development of people and help them be the best they can be. Then you recognize their qualities, and establish their development on recognized talents, and communicate their limitations with no restrictions.

- When you act as a leader from the position of love, you constantly question yourself and whether you are acting from the position of love.

And, of course, when you act from the position of love, then you get the car you deserve and drive it happily.

People also need the emotional part, but too much emotion or too many wrong and uncontrolled emotions, as well as any general lack of emotion, can lead to psychosis in both the individual and the entire organization. People need positive emotions to be balanced with the rational.

At the beginning of this book, it was mentioned that there are at least two reasons that people cannot and should not be treated in the mechanical way used when managing other resources.

Unlike all the resources (or assets) you manage (means, tools, finances, raw materials, facilities, plants, etc.), you cannot lead or manage people according to the same principles you use to manage other assets for two basic reasons: people are the only asset that have a brain and a heart. Respect that.

Lead people with the maximum balance between the rational and the emotional, and you will not go wrong.

I wish my boss was like that!

Because you certainly are.

References

As stated at the beginning, this book is a result of 20 long years of experience and all the events, people, and materials that occurred in that period and due to which these thoughts, ideas, facts, and projections are as they are. It is a result of everything learnt at and "stolen" from the Zagrebačka Banka, DHL, British American Tobacco and Coca-Cola, all the conversations, materials and experiences collected from numerous dear clients, people, and events whose names have been forgotten. However, the names of some people from whom valuable information and knowledge were obtained are: Pam Welsby, Syd Farley, Richard Finn, and Paul Dale-Harris.

In this book, there is certainly a thought, example, idea, or figure also stemming from these sources, and I offer my apologies for not having specified them; memory and oblivion are to blame for that, not intention. Meanwhile, the following sources have polished the book in certain ways:

Ardichvili, A and Kuchinke P. K, (2002) Leadership Styles and Cultural Values Among Managers and Subordinates: A Comparative Study of Four Countries of the Former Soviet Union, Germany, and the US, Human Resources Development International, 5:1, 99-117.

Berson, Y., Oreg, S. and Dvir, T., (2005) Organizational Culture Aa A Mediator Of CEO Values And Organizational Performance, Academy of Management Best Conference Paper.

Biddle, I, (2005) Approaches to Management: Style of Leadership, Business Date, Vol 13, No 3, 1-4.

Brent, M. (2002) Coaching for Development, The Ashridge Journal, 11-15.

Chamorro-Premuzic, T. and Furnham, A., (2010) The Psychology of Personnel Selection, Cambridge University Press.

Chang, A., McDonald, P. and Burton P., (2010) Methodological Choices in Work-Life Balance Research 1987 to 2006: A Critical Review, The International Journal of Human Resource Management, Vol. 21, No. 13, 2381-2413.

CIPD (2006), Coaching Supervision Maximizing The Potential Of Coaching, Chartered Institute of Personnel and Development.

CIPD (2010), The Talent Perspective: What Does It Feel Like To Be Talent Managed?, Survey Report, Chartered Institute of Personnel and Development.

CIPD (2010), A barometer of HR trends and prospects 2011, Survey Report, Chartered Institute of Personnel and Development.

Collins, J., (2001) Good To Great: Why Some Companies Make The Leap... And Others Don't, Harper Business.

Collins, R, (2004) Update on Leadership, AGSM magazine, Issue 3, 1-3.

Conceicao, S.C.O. and Altman, B.A., (2011) Training and Development Process and Organizational Culture Change, Organization Development Journal, Vol 9, Number 1, 33-43.

Daniels, A.C., (2000) Bringing Out The Best In People: How To Apply The Astonishing Power of Positive Reinforcement, McGraw-Hill.

Dewhurst, M., Guthridge, M. and Mohr, E. (2009) Motivating people: Getting beyond money, McKinsey & Company.

Drucker, P.F. (2001) The Essential Drucker (5ᵗʰ edition), Harper Business.

Fatt, J, (2004) Leadership Styles Between Technical and Non-technical Superiors: Guess Who Will Give Subordinates More Freedom on the Job?, Journal of Technical Writing and Communication, 34, 91-111.

Flood, P. C. at all (2000) Chief Executive Leadership Style, Consensus Decision Making, and Top Management Team Effectiveness, European Journal of Work and Organizational Psychology, Vol 9, No 3, 401-420.

Hersey, R.E., Blanchard, K.H. and Jonson, D.E., (2001) Management of Organizational Behavior: Leading Human Resources (8ᵗʰ edition), Prentice Hall.

Hrebiniak, L.G., (2005) Making Strategy Work: Leading Effective Execution And Change, Soundview Executive Book Summaries.

Jung, T., Scott, T., Davies, H.T.O., Bower, P., Whalley, D., MCNally, R. and Mannion, R., (2009) Instruments for Exploring Organizational Culture: A Review of the Literature, Public Administration Review, 1087-1096.

McCall, M. W. Jr, (2004) Leadership Development Through Experience, Academy of Management Executive, Vol 18, No 3, 127-130.

Mishel, L. and Davis, A., (2014) CEO Pay Continues To Rise As Typical Workers Are Paid Less, Economic Policy Institute, Issue Brief 380.

Muster V. and Schrader U., (2011) Green Work-Life Balance: A New Perspective for Green HRM, German Journal of Research in Human Resource Management, 25(2), 140-156.

Ogbonna, E. and Harris, L. C, (2000) Leadership Style, Organizational Culture and Performance: Empirical Evidence from UK Companies, International Journal of Human Resources Management, 11:4, 766-788.

Schwartz, J., Bersin, J. and Pelster B. (eds.) (2014), Global Human Capital Trends: Engaging The 21-century Workforce, Deloitte University Press.

Sinek, S., (2009) Start With Why: How Great Leaders Inspire Everyone To Take Action, Portfolio.

Smith, L. R., (2006) Leadership and Managing Thought, Journal of Innovative Management, 47-64.

Strack, R., Caye, J-M., Leicht, M.,Villis, U., Bohm, H. and McDonnell, M. (2012) The Future of HR in Europe: Key Challenged Through 2015, The Boston Consulting Group.

Sutherland, M. and Wocke, A., (2011) The Symptoms of And Consequences To Selection Errors in Recruitment Decisions, South African Journal of Business Management, 42 (4), 23-32.

Towers Watson, (2012) The Next High-Stakes Quest: Balancing Employer And Employee Priorities, 2012-2013 Global Talent Management And Reward Study, Towers Watson.

Trompenaars F. and Hampden-Turner C., (2004) Managing People Across Cultures, Capstone.

Weightman, J., (2008) Managing People, Chartered Institute of Personnel and Development.

Index

7S, 61

Attracting
  EVP, 97–107
  Lack of people, 94–96

Behaviors
  Culture, 66
  Value, 35

Candidates
  Communication channels,
    115–21
  Employment agencies, 110–
    12
  Information about, 107–10
  Resume, 110–12, 121–22

Capabilities, key (strategic)
  organizational, 152

Coaching
  As a process, 180–87
  As a system in organization,
    203–6
  GROW, 187

How to conduct, 187
  When to use, 187

Competences
  Attitudes, 154
  Behaviors, 152
  Development, 152
  Education, 153
  Emotions, 154
  Experience, 162
  Knowledge, 167
  Managerial skills, 154
  Soft, 154
  Technical, 193

Culture
  Behavior, 75–77
  Emergence, 58–63
  Kotter, about culture, 82–
    83
  Leader's influence, 67–77
  Management and
    Maintenance, 67–77

Measurement, 77–81
Organizational, 77–81
Power of, 64–67
Structure, 70
Success, 73
Tailor-made approach and
instruments, 87–92
Values, 73–75
Development
Action/project debriefing,
178
Assignment, 177–78
Behavior, change, 195
Climate for development,
200, 201
Coaching, 180–87
Competences, 109
E-learning (M-learning),
171–73
Environment for, 169
Feedback, 188–91
Market visit, 173
Measurement, 195–201
Mentoring, 179–80
Needs, 193
Peer development, 174–75
Position swapping, 175–77
Project participation, 174
Seminars, 170
Talents, 198
Techniques and Tools, 165–
79
Training, 170
Workshops, 170
Development measurement
Baseline measurement, 195
Measuring changes in
behavior, 197
Measuring knowledge, 196
Measuring satisfaction, 196
emotions, 111, 113, 117, 122
Employee Value Proposition
(EVP), 97–107
Employer branding, 104–7
Feedback, 188–91
Hertzberg
Hygiene factors, 30
Motivators, 30
Interview
Listening, 127
Questioning, 127
Selection, 135
STAR, 136–40
Leadership
Influencing skill, 16
Vs management, 18–23
Life-work balance
Vs Work-life balance, 45–50
Management
Vs Leadership, 18–23
Maslow
Esteem and recognition, 35
Hierarchy of needs, 31
Physiological needs, 31
Safety, 31
Self-actualization, 31
Social needs, 31
Mind, 38, 88
Motivation
Communication, 36
Exerting additional efforts,
37
Hertzberg, 30

Hygiene factors, 34, 35
Inclusion (feeling of), 38
Maslow, 30–35
Money, 39
Purpose and context, 38
Recognition, 35
Setting goals, 37
Motivators
Communication, 36
Exerting additional efforts, 37
Inclusion (feeling of), 38
Money, 39
Purpose and context, 38
Recognition, 35
Setting goals, 37
Punishment, 43–45
Recognition
Desired behaviors, 76
Evaluation and,, 75

Recruiting, 107, 115, 152
Selecting
Behaviors, 101
Job requirements, 121
Organizational culture fit, 80
Techniques and Methods, 121
Values, 100
Talents
Development, 191
Nine grid box, 193
Recognition, 193
Values
Branding, 62
Communication, 75
Counter-values, 62
Definition, 61
W-methodology, 78

Made in the USA
Coppell, TX
01 February 2022

72820661R00128